Displaying Qualitative Data

Peter Dahler-Larsen

Displaying Qualitative Data

University Press of Southern Denmark

© Peter Dahler-Larsen
Displaying Qualitative Data
Translated by Helene Pristed Nielsen
Prepress and Printing by Narayana Press 2008

ISBN 978-87-7674-377-2

University Press of Southern Denmark
Campusvej 55, 5230 Odense M
Tlf. 66 15 79 99 Fax 66 15 81 26
press@forlag.sdu.dk
www.universitypress.dk

Contents

The Iroquois' new Clothes – an Appetizer 7
The nameless Iroquois 8
European projections 9
The barelegged Iroquois 11
Saint-Sauveur and his fantastic project 12

The Importance of Displaying Data 15
Why are qualitative data often given too little attention? 18
Qualitative method today 20
Why link up with the practical methodological work on data? 22

The Importance of Rules for Displaying Data 24
Qualitative research 24
Why use qualitative method? 25
Data in qualitative research 28
Displaying qualitative data 28
Rules for displaying qualitative data 29

Displaying Data 32
Taking stock 32
Displays 37
The rule of authenticity 39
The rule of inclusion 42
The rule of transparency 45
First example: Studying a strike at SAS 46
Second example: Organisational structures within Bordurian agriculture ... 50
Third example: How shop stewards use the word 'democracy' 54
Fourth example: General practitioners' use of a new preventive treatment .. 56
Summing up on the displays 58
Do not forget the anomalies! 60
Asymmetrical displays 61
Drawing conclusions from displays 62
How a display fits into the research process 63

Negotiating the birth and design of an inquiry 64
Access, relations, and selection 66

Quality Criteria in Qualitative Inquiries 73
The characteristics of qualitative inquiries – a flow sheet 73
Quality criteria in qualitative inquiries 79
The correspondence criterion 79
The replication criterion 79
The reliability criterion 80
Communicative validity 81
Validity through good craftsmanship 83
The transparency criterion 84
The heuristic criterion 85
Pragmatic validity 86

Contingency and Rigour in Knowledge Production 88
Contingency 88
The active role of consciousness in knowledge production 90
Statements expressed by consciousness are untrustworthy 91
Language contributes to understanding 91
Meaning and understanding 93
Signification systems are relative to time and space 94
'Truth' as an institutional product 95
The sociology of knowledge makes knowledge relative 96
Scientific criticism of science 96
Doubt and reflexivity 97
The inherent logic of linguistic presentation 97
Contingency in the scientific approach to the empirical 99
Rigour 102
Rigour in analysing meaning 105
The connection between contingency and rigour 107
Active perspectivism 108
Contingent rigour and rigorous contingency 109

Summary 111

References 115

The Iroquois' new Clothes – an Appetizer

> *He thinks hunting and war the only cares worthy of a man. Therefore the Indian in the miserable depths of his forests cherishes the same ideas and opinions as the medieval noble in his castles, and he only needs to become a conqueror to complete the resemblance. How odd is it that the ancient prejudices of Europe should reappear, not among the European population along the coast, but in the forests of the new world.*
>
> (Tocqueville, 1978)

> *Savageness and civilisation are irretrievably linked. One does not exist without the other. The savages cannot know that they are savage without having been described by the civilised. And conversely, the civilised cannot know that they are civilised without the descriptions of the savages.*
>
> (Kjærsgaard, 1991: 2)[1]

'Grand Chef de Guerriers Iroquois' the inscription says. It is the great chief of the Iroquois warriors who is displayed on the cover of this book. I bought the original engraving from 1796 in a small shop in the Latin Quarter of Paris. The shop fascinated me; they only sold old engravings depicting animals, plants, body parts from a medical atlas, ethnographic engravings, and, above all, geographic maps – all dating from an era when the West thought itself capable of mapping and depicting the entire world adequately and precisely.

I never doubted the authenticity of the engraving; the shopkeeper's calm expression of expertise and professional pride added to my comfort. He spoke just about as little of all the languages of the world jointly as I spoke French. But he showed me in a reference book that the engraver, J. Grasset de Saint-Sauveur, actually was in North America at the end of the 18th century – at least as far as I understood.

---

1 Quote from Kannibaler, Stofskifte 15.

Both the engraver and the graphic adapter, J. Laroque, have signed the work. On the passepartout, the shopkeeper has added some information in pencil, such as the date 1796 and the first name of the engraver. The initial J. apparently stands for Jacques.

The nameless Iroquois

The great Iroquois chief, however, is displayed without a name. In his right hand, he is holding something which might be a war club, in his left apparently a pipe, which has been decorated to look like tomahawk. He is wearing a jacket and a triangular hat, which undoubtedly are of French origin. He is wearing a large medal around his neck. Proudly standing erect with one leg in front of the other, he is obviously striking a posture. He is standing there to be noticed. Behind him, you can see a house with a palisade around it. We cannot tell whether it is his own house or a French construction.

We ask ourselves: did the great Iroquois chief look like this? Grasset de Saint-Sauveur certainly came to North America, but did he actually see the chief and see him pose? Did Saint-Sauveur force, entice, persuade, or manipulate the Iroquois chief to pose in a French outfit, supplemented by various accessories? Or was the Iroquois himself perhaps fascinated by being depicted in foreign costume? Did he receive the jacket, hat, and medal from the French as a gift, perhaps in return for posing for the engraving or for something else?

Fur trade was a prime concern for the Europeans at the time. It is said that the Native Americans, prior to a proper deal insisted on sharing a good pipe of tobacco and exchange gifts. Maybe the chief has received the hat and medal on such an occasion?

The Iroquois lived in the area surrounding what is today Montreal and were whirled into the armed conflict between the English and French – how and when? There are issues that need to be clarified. How has Le Grand Chef de Guerriers Iroquois been constructed as a persona in this French-Native American play? Who benefits from displaying him in this posture? How did the Native American himself relate to the French and their equipment?

The French traits in the engraving of the posing chief with jacket, hat, and medal are easily recognisable. The pose and the perspective denotes a particular way of *displaying* this chief. But how does the display relate to the depiction – and the construction? What greater story is our friend Grasset de Saint-Sauveur telling us?

European projections

Maybe the history of a certain European image of the Native American is irretrievably linked with the era and the perspective. The Europeans create an image of *the Other* as an antithetical identity in relation to the Western one – sometimes in the form of stories about (Western) civilisation as a constant refinement of humanity, sometimes in the form of stories about the decadence of the West and what might be learned from 'man in his natural stage' – or whatever stories would fit into one's general scheme[2]. It is only at surface level that these stories are stories about *the Other*, ultimately these stories always turn out to be about the West itself.

A set of tacit cultural assumptions are being reproduced, *implicit understandings* (Stuart Schwartz in Liebersohn, 1998: 9) or what Umberto Eco (1998) calls *background books.*

The Iroquois are easy to fit into these background books. The Iroquois appear almost magnetically attractive in relation to European images. The Iroquois are tall, brave, and proud. The Iroquois raise their children without using force. The Iroquois declare war and negotiate peace on the basis of a dignified consensual process. The Iroquois display an interesting and complex political structure, whose foundation rests on a principle of representation, ensuring that the rulers at all times will express the general will of the Iroquois nation (Liebersohn, 1998: 13-14).

It is easy to trace a reflection of Enlightenment notions of coinciding reason and nature in the depiction. But it is not *only* a question of simple transferral of Western cognitive patterns on the foreigners. The Europeans, and not least the French, themselves have their own need for putting forward models of lawmaking and political authority which might pose alternatives to the existing monarchy that burdens the entire society. (The argument about innate human reason forms a convenient counterpoint: it serves to explain why equality and reason constitute arguments for a modern political order).

Therefore, it comes as no surprise that the following has been written about the Iroquois form of government: *'The form of government has a simplicity and*

---

2 Just like Tocqueville saw noble traits in the Indians, Engels (1884/1970) finds communist ones: 'No soldiers, no gendarmes, no police, and no nobles, kings, bureaucrats or judges, no prisons, no courts. Nobody can be poor or suffering – the community and the family recognise their responsibility to the old, the sick, and the invalids. All are equal and free, including the women. You can tell how much men and women in such a community have achieved from the admiration awoken in all those white people who have not been demoralised, and you can tell from the personal dignity, justice, strength of character, and courage marking these savages'.

at the same time a wisdom that our profound legislators have not yet been able to achieve in their sophisticated codes (...) Is it necessary then to go to the Iroquois to find a model of legislation?'. And who is the originator of this question?

Actually, it is no less than the master himself responsible for the picture of the grand Iroquois chief, our friend J. Grasset de Saint-Sauveur. Saint-Sauveur asks the question in a work about attires from the entire world, but in true encyclopaedic spirit he touches upon one thing and another in relation to the various peoples of the world. The work has been published twice, in 1784 and 1788 – that is, immediately prior to the French Revolution (Liebersohn 1998: 13). In it, Grasset airs his subversive Enlightenment ideas more or less directly.

Following the Revolution, the balance in the history of ideas shifts from Enlightenment to Romanticism. This also entails a shift in the background books which define what is written between the lines in the descriptions of the Native Americans. Now the Iroquois chiefs are considered to possess courage, dignity, grandeur, and generosity.

The Europeans increasingly depict the Native Americans as extraordinarily tall and proud. They are proud hunters and warriors, despising manual labour. They are elegant in their behaviour and dress, and their self-respect is excessive.[3]

What do they remind us of? They remind us of the nobility whose values are on the retreat within European culture exactly towards the end of the 18th century.

'The noble savage' has, in addition to his conventional significance, acquired a secondary significance as 'the savage nobility'. It is a figure the European makes use of to remind himself of a nostalgic loss of values. There are certain ideas about dignity, bravery, chivalry, the sovereign ability to rise above the trivial, and, above all, having pride as one's guiding principle in life, which have only been realised within European culture through the existence of our nobility. But times are changing. The heads of the nobility are rolling, and the advance of equality is manifesting itself as an unavoidable historical tendency (Tocqueville, 1978).

The dominant American culture, with its focus on the practical, its vulgar fixation on wealth, and its narrow-minded focus on the values of a society based on equality, is interpreted by European observers as a forewarning about the inevitability of modernity – also in Europe (Tocqueville, 1978). Meanwhile, the Native American is becoming an object of shifting European projections; not projections of what there is, or what there will be, but projections of what is

---

3 Knudsen in Weekendavisen, 8-14 October 1999 in the article 'Noble Savages', a review of Harry Liebersohn (1998).

being lost. Both as a consequence of and a reaction to the Enlightenment belief in reason, Romanticism is making its impact on Europe; and this facilitates an idealisation of the noble savage as the antithesis of modernity. During Romanticism, people long for 'the good old days' of the authentic, the emotional, the natural, and the harmonic, the noble.

Because of this longing, Europeans start seeing the Natives in a different light. While the Iroquois during the reign of Enlightenment ideals has to be depicted as a model for democracy, he is on the contrary seen as a model for aristocratic values during the influence of Romanticism. These are the main features of Liebersohn's (1998) analysis of European projections on Native Americans.[4]

It is impossible to interpret the description of the Iroquois as a statement about the Iroquois warrior himself, without simultaneously interpreting the description as a statement about the way the Iroquois is *displayed*. It is the background books of Grasset de Saint-Sauveur and the entire historic and cultural constellation behind this presentation which condition this posture, this hat, this jacket, this medal.

The barelegged Iroquois

'You missed something', two women, who ordinarily work with pictures, exclaimed upon hearing my presentation and interpretation of the Iroquois.[5]

'Look down! You missed the fact that he isn't wearing any trousers', one of them said. His bare legs reveal something. Maybe he thought that only his torso would be visible in the engraving. Maybe the Iroquois chief himself did not find his bare legs significant, maybe he thought it quite uncomplicated. But within the grander scheme of things, with the chief posing as a figure of authority, the bare legs reveal the artificial nature of the entire tableau. Thus exposing the Iroquois, Jacques Grasset de Saint-Sauveur also exposes his own depiction of the Native American.

---

4 How was it possible – two completely different descriptions of the same reality? Iroquois forms of government were complex enough to support more than one interpretation of values (Liebersohn, 1998: 20), and in addition, as Liebersohn writes (1998: 35), some of the descriptions of Native Americans had 'lost their relationship to any reality, European or American'.

5 A special thanks to documentary film director Ulla Boye Rasmussen and graphic artist Inge Lise Westman for watching, listening, and commenting with great attention at San Cataldo, 13 December 2000.

Maybe I had been too preoccupied with decoding Saint-Sauveur's background books to take notice of my own, and at the same time I had forgotten one of the *first simple principles of the qualitative inquiry: look carefully.*

It is a fictive tableau, with the Native chief promptly posing in various costumes, but the depiction – of the bare legs, which, after all, are in the picture – shows us something. The presentation is the result of a history. The same is true for those aspects of the presentation we are prone to overlook as well.

What do we actually know about the encounter between the great Iroquois chief and J. Grasset de Saint-Sauveur?

Saint-Sauveur and his fantastic project

We would have liked to know what the Iroquois chief himself had to say about the matter. But apart from his appearance as Grand Chef de Guerriers Iroquois, he is excluded from our history. He is nameless; we do not know his language. The livelihood of his people is being undermined, while Europe is taking over world history; a process that is already well under way while Grasset de Saint-Sauveur is depicting those people who will lose out to history. So there are limits to what we can demand from the Iroquois chief.

Grasset de Saint-Sauveur, on the other hand, might have given us a little more. He could have told us why the Iroquois chief in this particular engraving is wearing a jacket and a hat, and whether it was suggested to him that he should strike a pose. However, Grasset de Saint-Sauveur died a long time ago. In 1810.

The single most important help towards acquiring a reasonable understanding of the production history of the engraving, however, has been provided by our friend Grasset by virtue of his signature.

Jacques Grasset de Saint-Sauveur was born in Montreal in Canada in 1757.[6] His father worked as a secretary to the Governor of the French possessions. In 1764, little Jacques – seven years old – left Canada in a hurry to return to France with his family, because his father had become involved in a court case. This was just one year prior to the French giving up Canada to the British. Having attended school in Paris, Jacques, with the help of his father, entered on a diplomatic career. Among other appointments, he became a vice consul in Hungary during unspecified periods. He has been described as a man possessing few original thoughts and an artists without a talent. With great devotion and enthusiasm he covered many fields of interest, publishing a love story and conducting a theatre ensemble.

---

6 www.unites.uqam.ca

But to return to his graphic works. I have already touched upon his work about the attires of the peoples of the world from 1784-88. Another major publication, containing 432 coloured engravings and running to five volumes, is issued in 1795-96. It is *'Encyclopedie de voyages, contenant l'abrégé historique des moeurs, usages, habitudes domestiques, religions, fêtes, supplices, funérailles, sciences et arts et commerce de tout les peuples et la collection complete de leurs habillement civil, militaries, religieux et dignitaries dessines, desinnés d'apres nature. Gravés avec soin, et coloriés a l'aquarelle'.*

It is an ambitious project Grasset de Saint-Sauveur is undertaking here. *'Tout les peuples'* – *all peoples* are described, and this is both with regard to customs, religions, celebrations, sufferings, funerals, science, art, trade, plus a complete collection of their attires, both civilian, military, and religious. One may wonder how Grasset has managed to cover all this, and even draw everything 'after nature', even if he did receive help from among others J. Laroque with the job of afterwards carefully engraving and then colouring all the illustrations. In the volume on America alone, 26 peoples are described using 92 illustrations. What a tremendous undertaking it must have been in the 18th century to visit 26 different peoples in North America and get to know them well enough to describe all these aspects of their lives!

It gives even greater cause for wonder when you consider the fact that already in 1798, only two or three years later, he publishes another major work, this time surveying the most important peoples of Europe, Asia, Africa, and America, in addition giving an account of the discoveries by Captain Cook, La Perouse, and others. Did Grasset de Saint-Sauveur manage to follow in the footsteps of Cook *and* pay a thorough visit to at least four continents in such a short time?

Maybe it is more likely that he sometimes has been drawing away with his motive only appearing before his mind's eye. What has he been basing his depictions on, if it is only second or third hand information he received? His comprehensive encyclopaedic quest to map almost all details about all peoples – 'tous les peuples' feeds into our sneaking suspicion that the project is impossible, and that there is a very weak link, indeed, between each of his illustrations and the reality they purport to present. Maybe Grasset never forced, enticed, persuaded, or manipulated any Iroquois person to pose for him. Maybe the way the Iroquois chief is displayed is a product of Grasset's imagination which has been transposed to paper. Did he even set foot in Canada after leaving at the age of seven?

Harry Liebersohn is very clear in his analysis of the circumstances surrounding the productions of Jacques Grasset de Saint-Sauveur: *'He did not seem to be travelling at all, just idealizing European qualities and wrapping them up in native costume. In his illustrations the Iroquois man fits heroic or even godlike conventions of European art ... These 'Indians' look at first sight like Frenchmen in drag'* (Liebersohn, 1998: 14).

We are unlikely ever to get a full picture of the production conditions relating to Grasset's images. But we have gained considerable insight since we started out. It proved helpful to take a look at the background books. It proved helpful to take a look at the bare legs in the actual display. And even if Grasset has not been very helpful in providing information about the circumstances of how his image has been produced, he has in fact done us a great favour in signing the work. This has made it possible for us to draw certain conclusions.

Make your displays in a systematic way. And always sign your work.

> Some years after the publication of the first edition of this book, I strolled around the Latin Quarter in Paris. Miraculously, I stumbled over another engraving by Saint-Sauveur. This time, the display presented the "Roi de Juida", the king of Whidah, or Oudah, a city in present Benin, historically notoriously famous for its port and its slave trade. Like the Iroquois, this noble man is wearing a long, green coat – and bare legs. Continents apart, both are "Frenchmen in drags". Both appear to be similar projections of Saint-Sauveurs imagination. Now, we are even less willing to believe that Saint-Sauveur's displays were drawn "after nature."

CHAPTER 1
The Importance of Displaying Data

Earlier, ethnographers and anthropologists travelled to foreign shores to find forms of life they could wonder about. Today, they will inquire into work training programmes for long term unemployed people in Bradford, study teenagers' substance abuse, or the organisational culture of a government department.

Many other people and organisations make use of types of inquiry that are similar to those of ethnographers and anthropologists. Social scientific research, applied research, public inquiries, evaluations, and consultancy reports together make up a mixture of forms of knowledge production which concern themselves with our society and its problems.

Within this mixture, qualitative research methods have in recent times become remarkably widespread. Social scientific research based on qualitative methods has become a prime factor in the way our societies describe themselves. Qualitative method has become an *applied* method. Universities teach qualitative method as a subject that no longer is associated with revolutionary tendencies. Hundreds of students are each year sent into the field to undertake qualitative inquiries in areas such as management, organisation, marketing, and social work. Marketing gurus and political spin doctors strive to be the first to use the latest ideas within qualitative method. Evaluators have been using qualitative method for some time, and consultancy firms working with organisational change today apply qualitative methods with great familiarity.

Qualitative method is used when one seeks to understand the relation between social workers and clients, between doctors and patients, between teachers and pupils. Qualitative method is used when one seeks to understand complicated relationships between substance abuse and crime. Qualitative method is used when one seeks to chart the knowledge about AIDS among prostitutes, in order to plan a better information campaign to reach them (Manata et al. 1991). Qualitative method is used to describe people's feelings about quickset hedges in order to take account of these in landscape planning (Oreszczyn and Lane, 2000). Qualitative method is used to study how patients experience hospital treatment to see if improvements can be made.

Qualitative methods of inquiry ask questions, point out problems, clear front pages, give a voice to the silenced ones, count as documentation, and incite political action.

Qualitative inquiries, however, also contain a set of particular methodological problems. In principle, a qualitative inquiry is sensitive towards the particular cultural context in which it is being applied. In principle, the aim is to capture facts that are different, surprising, cross-cutting, unusual, and/or culturally specific in relation to what you would expect. Qualitative methods can observe with wonder the exotic within the ordinary. A primary aspect in the definition of qualitative method is exactly the fact that the most important categories of the inquiry have not been predetermined by the researcher. (They are predetermined in a quantitative inquiry, where you have to assume that you know what you want to measure).

For this reason, qualitative inquiries always operate with a more or less flexible design. The methods for data collection and the way of asking questions can be developed as the inquiry comes along. The qualitative inquiry is less programmable and less regulated in its approach compared to quantitative inquiries.

Many qualitative inquiries run into a set of foreseeable problems. To give a brief list, these problems include: A lot of data is collected, but it is difficult to structure it. The actual analysis is begun too late, and is influenced more by practical limitations in terms of time and feasibility than by an analytic goal. The analysis is based on illuminating selective pickings from data. It is difficult to follow the trail of evidence from method to data to conclusion.

Example of an inquiry where it is difficult to trace the road from data to conclusion:

On 4 April 2001, the Danish newspaper Politiken published a report from ECRI (European Commission against Racism and Intolerance). The report gives a rather negative picture of the situation concerning racism, xenophobia, and intolerance in Denmark (Politiken, 2001).

Obviously, the report sparked a debate, even if many of the standpoints were quite predictable.

Central passages of the report were based on a number of vague and obscure formulations, such as 'it does not seem that...', 'certain parts of Danish society...', 'widespread accounts...', and 'some media...' – all without any further clarification or indication of the source.

This blurred relationship between data and conclusion made it relatively easy to criticise the report and dismiss it, if one already from the outset opposed its ideas.

ECRI inquires into each country according to a certain cycle. On 16 May 2006 it was again Denmark's turn to be subject to a report. ECRI had not made any fundamental changes to its research methods. This time, too, there are problems with undocumented and imprecise formulations. One of the most obvious ones being 'ECRI is profoundly concerned over reports that certain judges are prejudiced against witnesses and defendants of ethnic minority background' (ECRI 2006: 12).

If these reports are correct, it would be a giant blow to the integrity of the Danish judicial system. But because the reports are indeterminate and no source is given, and because 'certain judges' are not further defined, the reader is left with only baseless accusations.

Immediately following the publication of the report, Prime Minister Anders Fogh Rasmussen was ready with harsh criticism. A large part of the following debate turned on the poor quality of the report rather than on racism, xenophobia, and intolerance in Denmark. As these questions in any case are politically charged in Denmark, the report was likely to have come under fire in all events. But if ECRI's research methods had been reliable, the report was likely to have fared better in this debate. Applying a more rigorous method, ECRI could have made life harder for its opponents. Instead, life was made easy for the opponents, and the actual observations in the report were never discussed, even if ECRI did put forward relevant points and recommendations.

Students, consultants, and researchers – as well as readers of their inquiries – often experience these problems as very real.[1]

Students often encounter great problems when trying to structure and report on their qualitative inquiries. They are often left with the experience that everything happens too late – especially the analysis. This results in reports where many pages are taken up by the introduction, the premises, the choice of theory, methodological problems, problems with access to the field, etc. Time, energy, and pages run out before getting to the actual analysis. The submitted report turns out *front-heavy*: it never becomes a seaworthy project, because all the weight is placed at the front of the vessel.

---

1 This is an 'impression'. This book in itself is not a qualitative inquiry, but a description of methodological rules. The book is not intended to illustrate its own rules, just like a menu card is not meant to be eaten.

Consultants sometimes deliver reports containing wide-ranging recommendations where it might be difficult to see the connection to data, among other things because these are not reported in a systematic manner.

Researchers also sometimes express frustrations about the qualitative research process. Off-camera, they describe the qualitative research process as overwhelming, and reveal that there are great differences between the official methodological rules of the game on the one hand, and actual practice on the other (van Maanen, 1988).

This book is intended for all qualitative researchers and users of qualitative inquiries, be they researchers, evaluators, consultants, and not least students, whose qualitative research competences are undergoing development. The book is intended for everyone who finds it worrying if weak qualitative inquiries start setting the agenda for how to handle certain problems in our society.

It is worthwhile asking the question why the above mentioned problems with data, data treatment, and reporting often occur in qualitative inquiries, and, in extension of this, obviously asking whether anything can be done differently while still paying heed to the specific methodological characteristics of qualitative inquiries. Great inherent problems that are incurable to boot should not characterise qualitative method. It is one thing if the problems occur by accident or pure inattention. It is another and far graver matter if there are systematic reasons for these problems.

Why are qualitative data often given too little attention?

I have in different connections heard the following *four arguments for not subjecting data treatment and reporting in qualitative inquiries to careful systematisation*. None of them are good. But let us take a look at them one by one.

The first argument is that there are restrictions on the time and resources available for qualitative inquiries. Therefore, there is simply not enough time to be very thorough in the treatment and analysis of data. This argument does not hold sway. It would for example be possible to choose a smaller set of data and be more rigorous when treating it. Time and resources are always limited, and therefore this is not a good argument for one concrete methodological decision rather than another. A central ingredient in displaying methodological skill is to be able to choose the best possible course of action given the available time and resources.

A second argument is that people who commission a qualitative inquiry set up certain demands. For example, consultancy companies sometimes find that companies commissioning a large inquiry have as one of their selection criteria how many qualitative interviews are carried out when specifying conditions for tenders; disregarding how data is being treated. This might be a real problem. But in that case, it is based on a social construction which is not pre-given. Criteria for choosing between tenders can be influenced, among other things, by education. Consultancy companies themselves can influence quality criteria in their work by the way they argue in their bid to undertake the inquiry, through concrete research results, and by marketing competitive ways of treating data. The argument is a reflection of the fact that quality criteria within qualitative inquiries can have a marked social and institutional basis, without adding anything to their scientific quality.

A third argument – common among students – is that all forms of interpretation ultimately are subjective. Therefore it seems unnecessary to systematise data treatment to any great degree. However, this argument lands you in trouble if there are no limitations at all to the rampage of subjectivism within scientific work.

A fourth argument is that rigour and rules for data treatment are an external and boring nuisance which is a remnant of other times and obsolete methodological schools, and does not belong in contemporary qualitative method. Rigour and rules are considered educational dictates – something one has to be examined in – things learned by rote. Old-fashioned and boring teaching in methodology presents method as a set of external rules one has to live up to, and not as a practical skill it is worthwhile for the researcher to acquire for his or her own benefit and enjoyment, nor as a practice which is directly related to the good inquiry itself. According to the self-understanding of the so-called 'progressive' qualitative method, the most important thing is to be as open as possible to unexpected impulses and surprising information – therefore, structures and rules for the collection and representation of data are considered dogmas, and antithetical to qualitative method as such. However, this argument is based on an illusion; the illusion that it is possible to remain open towards everything simultaneously.

These four arguments did not just appear out of nowhere. Particularly the last two arguments denote common perceptions by many who have been exposed to teaching qualitative method. It is likely that in the effort to emphasise the special character of qualitative method, some points have been overplayed. In combination with the underplaying of other equally relevant points, this has contributed to giving the students an unbalanced understanding of qualitative method, whose practical consequences have been unfortunate.[2]

Therefore, there might be a need to adjust and possibly revise the tenets

---

2 This must be worrisome for anyone teaching qualitative method. If the book in some places comes across as somewhat condescending in its educational tone, it is partly because the book is also a reminder to myself as a teacher in qualitative method.

of qualitative method – possibly the way they are taught, and certainly the way they are understood. Familiar doctrines about the researcher's openness towards the unexpected and the subjectivity of interpretations may need to be clarified, and, not least, be supplemented with tenets that may work as efficient counterpoints. Key words for some of these new tenets may be: rigour in the data analysis, bounding of data, displays that sum up and concentrate large amounts of data without showing only select pickings, data saturation, inference, and rules for displaying data.

I see a need for a discussion of these tenets, especially in the light of the recent changes in the practical social contexts in which qualitative inquiry is applied.

Qualitative method today

Unlike the familiar scenario in many research environments a few years ago, qualitative method is no longer above all a groundbreaking scientific rebellion which has to justify its existence via a militant battle of paradigms. The defence took the approach that if qualitative method may look like a lax methodological practice when measured by conventional standards, there are actually other scientific standards on whose basis qualitative method is well-founded. If qualitative method came under attack, the philosophy of science card was played. Evidently, it is important to define and reflect upon the different scientific paradigms which may lead to different varieties of qualitative inquiry, such as phenomenology and hermeneutics (Schwandt 2000).

Today, however, it may not be in this front, but in two other fronts, that the most decisive battles determining the future of qualitative methods take place.

One of these fronts is political. It is popular today to identify qualitative methods with a particular political agenda (Denzin and Lincoln 2000), but by mobilizing "us" against "them", advocates of qualitative method may become unreflective about their own problematic assumptions, and they may ignore the important critical contributions of others (Schwandt 2006). In addition, qualitative researchers may lose broad social acceptance of their findings because of their built-in political assumptions.

Another, but related front has to do with the practical quality of qualitative research. Today, qualitative methods are carried forward by their practical applicability and usefulness (Gibbons et al., 1994). The debate about qualitative methods does not only take place among philosophers of science, but to an increasing extent in a variety of practical social settings all over the world. Sometimes qualitative researchers find themselves in a "schizophrenic position" as they carry out interpretive research but feel confronted with claims from other, perhaps more powerful stakeholders, that their research be "rigorous scientific research" (for an example, see Scott and Oelofse 2007). It would be nice if qualitative researchers found practical ways to reduce the apparent contradiction between interpretive work and rigorous research.

However, as consultants, students, journalists, think tanks and government offices use qualitative methods in massive numbers, the attention to the quality of inquiry may be declining. In a time when qualitative method is becoming more widespread, it is of particular importance to discuss how we practice it, to problematise concrete approaches and ways of producing data, and not least to trace and trial the claims based on qualitative data in a critical way. If not, we risk reckless subjectivism in interpretations, jumping to conclusions, and undermining the critical public debate about methods and findings.

How we argue for, develop, and protect qualitative method depends on what we perceive as the greatest threats and challenges to it. We now risk that a continued banging of the war drums in the battle of paradigms will land us in a situation where we end up legitimising qualitative research of unnecessary poor quality.

You will find this book useful if you agree with me that attention to the practical quality of qualitative methods is of outmost importance.

If one aims for the insight, legitimation, and social accept emanating from scientific practice, one has to proceed by certain methodological principles. In qualitative methods, these are not easily defined. Nevertheless, the aim of this book is to suggest methodological rules for producing and displaying data, which one can follow in order to strengthen the scientific character of one's qualitative inquiry. Regardless of whether criticism of actual qualitative research is justified or not, practitioners of qualitative method may strengthen their position if they are able to explain clearly how they have collected, handled and interpreted data.

The suggestions in this book about how to do so constitute only a part of the work involved in a qualitative inquiry, but it is an important part, which may carry great implications for other parts of the work. However, the message of this book should be understood in the context of other messages about qualitative method, such as messages concerning the scientific basis of qualitative methodology (Schwandt, 2000), its history (Vidich and Lyman, 2000), ethical foundation, design (Maxwell, 1996), how it is tied up with social and organisational relations (Mirvis, 1985), power relations, quality criteria and validation (Denzin, 2000), problems of textual communication (Marcus and Fischer, 1986), and reporting (Richardson, 2000) and so on and so forth.

In this book, I keep a focus on *methodological rules for displaying data.* Such rules may improve qualitative inquiries as such. Students will experience that their reports will become less front-heavy and the actual analysis will take on a more prominent place. Consultants and readers of consultancy reports will experience that conclusions and recommendations will be more obviously grounded in and argued for from data.

Why link up with the practical methodological work on data?

The focal point for this entire book is the *practice of qualitative method.* I am interested in how qualitative method is *practiced*. There are three reasons for this.

The first reason is that a focus on the practice of qualitative inquiries will alleviate many recurring problems. A lot of the discourse surrounding qualitative method makes thinking and reflection, (and lately also) identity and 'being,' basic reference points in the methodological work. None of these are unimportant. But it is also worthwhile to focus on the actual practice – the doing of qualitative inquiry.

The second reason is that the practice of qualitative method has to be a source of major inspiration and at the same time work as a counterpoint to those aspects of methodological teaching we might call *normative methodology* – i.e. methodological rules for how one *ought* to carry out the work. A substantial number of books on methodology are purely based on normative methodology, and they tend to make the subject boring, barren, and unworldly, which the students might learn and reproduce, without actually linking it up with arguments about and within their own methodological practice. Normative methodology continually ought to be engaged in dialogue with and reflect on what we might term *descriptive methodology*, i.e. description of how social scientific method is in fact carried out in practice.

There is a gap between normative and descriptive methodology. Often, when researchers discuss among themselves, they readily acknowledge that this gap exists (van Maanen, 1988). It would be good frankly to admit the gap between these two, because it would contribute to keeping the methodological discussions and reflections alive. It is equally clear that as soon as you make suggestions within normative methodology, you are prone to the criticism that your own previous research does not live up to the suggested standards (this is the risk I run by writing this book!).

Just like moral guidelines may serve a relevant function as ideals, even if the actual actions of people in fact do not live up to them, normative methodology may have beneficial effects, even if the guidelines set up within it do not fully correspond with descriptive methodology. There has to be a dialogue between normative and descriptive method. It is not enough to formulate a formally correct and scientifically grounded normative methodology without considering the consequences for descriptive methodology. Equally, the practice of descriptive methodology should be of interest to normative methodology. Teaching qualitative method – including the way I have been teaching it myself – often operates with honourable doctrines based on a philosophical scientific approach, which, however, often end up being a little imprecisely formulated, left unchallenged, and often slightly misunderstood by the students. This has had unfortunate consequences for the actual inquiry practice. The presentation of qualitative data often lacks rigour. In my opinion, the same observation holds good for a substantial number of those qualitative inquiries that are today gaining importance for our society in the form of 'applied science', consultancy reports, evaluations, and so on.

This brings us to *the third reason* why we should be interested in the practice of qualitative method. It is of increasing relevance to society how qualitative inquiries are actually carried out and which recommendations are made on their basis; i.e. which claims are made in the name of qualitative inquiries. *Therefore, it is advisable to be interested in the practice of qualitative method, and, consequently, it is also worthwhile to let normative methodology confront these challenges.*

In chapter 2 below, I will give a closer account of the problem of setting up methodological rules for displaying data in qualitative inquiries, and include an analysis of each of the significant words in this way of stating the problem.

In chapter 3, I will come up with three concrete suggestions for displaying data in qualitative inquiries, namely the rule of authenticity, the rule of inclusion, and the rule of transparency. In addition, I will give four practical examples of how these rules may be applied when making displays, i.e. concentrated representations of qualitative data.

In chapter 4, I will argue for such a practice on the basis of various quality criteria for qualitative inquiries.

The last chapter 5 I will use to argue for my position on rules for displaying data in more general, philosophical scientific terms, namely as based on a relationship between contingency and rigour in the production of knowledge.[3] The book ends with a short summary on the usefulness of displays for both the reader and the researcher.

First of all, however, I wish to elaborate and argue for the aim of the book and its delimitation by discussing each of the significant words in the statement: to give suggestions to *methodological rules you can subject yourself to when displaying data in qualitative inquiries.*

---

3   This chapter was written first. But I changed the order of the chapters. I criticise many qualitative research reports for being front-heavy, so I have to ensure that my own book is not!

CHAPTER 2
The Importance of Rules for Displaying Data

Qualitative research

Qualitative method comprises a jumble of various types of studies, not only in the form of research (both basic research, applied research and sector research), but also in the form of expositions for think tanks, evaluations, organisational inquiries, consultancy inquiries, and student assignments. These have for all intents and purposes emerged as an identifiable category, and to a large extent they have cultivated a self-conception as *research based on qualitative method.*

The noun *research* means 'diligent and systematic inquiry or investigation into a subject in order to discover or revise facts, theories, applications, etc.'[1]

Qualitative research can be defined in various ways. It is defined in terms of its method, which can be approached on at least three different levels:

Figure 1: Three methodological levels:

- Method as philosophy of science: epistemology and ontology

- Method as logic of inquiry

- Method as technique and tool for treating and applying data

It would be possible to define qualitative method at the lowest level as a series of techniques for collecting data which is not comprised by numbers, i.e. which is not quantitative data. Following this approach, it is possible to speak about qualitative interviews without further consideration of the more general arguments for this entire logic of inquiry. However, if qualitative method is

---

1 Webster's Encyclopaedic Unabridged Dictionary of the English Language, Gramercy Books, New York. Revised edition, 1996.

defined merely at this lowest level, we will not learn much about the essence of qualitative method.

It would also be possible to define qualitative method on the basis of epistemological and ontological considerations at the higher level of philosophy of science. For example, it would be possible to base one's logic of inquiry and data collection techniques on a phenomenological or hermeneutical approach to the human being as a meaning-constructing creature (Schwandt 2000). Suspended in the webs of significance he/she himself has spun (Geertz 1975). It would even be possible to do so consistently. But this would not hit the nail on its head as far as the aim of this book is concerned. Even if 'qualitative method' historically has been more inspired by some positions rather than others within philosophy of science (for example phenomenology and hermeneutics), today it would not, in my opinion, be possible to define it wholly based on such a delimitation. It would be a pity if qualitative researchers were to reject otherwise fair methodological rules solely on the grounds that they do not adhere to the direction within philosophy of science from which the rule is derived. (This does not mean that the overall argument of this book is without its philosophical foundation, but more about this in chapter 5).

Being aware of both the advantages as well as disadvantages this implies, I will dare to define qualitative method neither at the technical level nor at the level of philosophy of science, but rather at the middle range level – the level of research logic. Here it is my claim that, at least ideally, qualitative method can be defined as follows:

Qualitative research operates with a flexible design, because the most important categories of the inquiry have not been predetermined by the researcher. On the contrary, categories are developed as a function of the actual research undertaken.

Why use qualitative method?

There can be three *reasons for not determining the categories of an inquiry in advance:*

1. The field of study is yet relatively unexplored.

2. The field of study is multiple and complex, consisting of disorganised structures of information etc.

3. The field of study is made up of cultural constructions, created by the field itself. These can by definition not be understood by the researcher before

the research has been undertaken. In the words of Zaner (1973): 'To seek to understand the social world as it is for those people whose social world it is, is possible only if one practices the art of listening to them in their own terms and attends to the social world they construct for themselves'. Therefore, the researcher has to navigate according to these constructions, rather than predetermine his or her research categories.

The first two of these reasons are situational: one's choice of qualitative method is dependent on aspects of the situation in which the inquiry takes place. Adherents of quite different paradigms can for good reasons opt for qualitative method or not; it depends on the situation.

The third reason is more general, of axiomatic and paradigmatic nature. If, for example, one takes a constructionist approach, any research situation would entail an interest in constructed social imaginary significations (Castoriadis, 1987), which determine a given social order. In such a case, the application of qualitative method is a logical consequence of the philosophical paradigm. Consequently, constructionists will, on the basis of reason number three, consistently select qualitative method independently of the given research situation.

It follows from the above that when both 1, 2, and 3 can be reasons for choosing qualitative method, the category of 'qualitative method' is not something that is practiced by people adhering to the same paradigm(s). As I intend to target exactly this category of research, qualitative method, I have not defined this category at the paradigmatic level.

On the other hand, it is a highly relevant agenda for social scientific method to take a stand on this category of research, because qualitative method in practice is becoming more widespread and more generally applied.

Qualitative research has transgressed former boundaries within philosophy of science, and today it much more resembles what Gibbons, Limoges, Nowotny, Schwartzman, Scott, and Trow (1994) call *knowledge production in Mode II*. In contrast with conventional scientific knowledge production, called Mode I, Mode II is usually localised directly within and organised in relation to a question of application, where several different categories of stakeholders within society are brought into play. This can for example be in the form of market inquiries, technology assessments, and evaluations.

The spread of knowledge production in Mode II is connected with the emergence of reflexive modernity in our societies. During the era of reflexive modernity, the major problems of society are neither effects of natural threats nor external enemies, but rather the unintended side-effects imposed on society through the use of complex technology and complex forms of organisation.

These side-effects are thrown back (reflected) on society itself, creating a need to relate a new to things and practices, and think about them in new ways (reflect) (Beck, 1994).

In the absence of clear normative ideals for the future, a political culture of doubt and critique is spreading. Qualitative method is used to make large organisations, which are otherwise more prone to talk than listen, adjust their antennas a little more towards receiving input. Qualitative method has proved useful as a tool for developing greater sensitivity in relation to unintended side-effects, the experience of risk, problems of coordination, and user reactions.

In this sense, the use of qualitative method pertains to how we handle joint societal problems. It is our concern how qualitative research describes our joint problems and which claims are made on the basis of results from qualitative inquiries.

Mode II knowledge production is by definition socially dispersed. The production of knowledge involves various types of stakeholders, which means that the knowledge produced should be held accountable to a set of socially defined validation criteria, besides the scientific ones. This can for example be demands for applicability, usefulness, profitability, levels of funding, social acceptability, and political correctness. Knowledge in Mode II has to meet social expectations in a broader sense than conventional Mode I knowledge production (Gibbons, Limoges, Nowotny, Schwartzman, Scott, and Trow 1994: 3). Under these circumstances, the rules guiding the creation of systematic knowledge are "up for graps".

This does not mean that people who produce Mode II knowledge cannot adhere to scientific criteria. In some cases, qualitative inquiries are clearly carried out as scientific work and validated as such. In other cases, the inquiry is not institutionally defined as 'research', but in connection with the social legitimacy and impact of the inquiry, it is emphasised that it has been carried out by a researcher or research institution and/or that it *moreover in its approach and terminology resembles scientific research.* When this happens, it is reasonable to demand scientific rigour in the methodological rules that have been applied. Finally, I want to claim that by adhering to a few simple rules in the production and presentation of qualitative data, one can greatly enhance the potential for new insights and the robustness of one's claims, independently of whether the actual inquiry is made within an explicitly scientific framework.

As already mentioned, demands for scientific character are not the only types of demands made on Mode II types of knowledge. However, the fact that demands for scientific character compete with other types of demands in a more complex and conflicting way in Mode II knowledge production compared to Mode I, makes it perhaps even more pertinent to draw attention to these scientific demands, including demands regarding the way data is treated.

Data in qualitative research

The word *data* has been chosen deliberately to emphasise that qualitative inquiries not only operate with impressions and interpretations, but also with data. The word data derives from the Latin word *datum*, which means 'given', that which is given (with certainty), which again derives from the verb *dare*, to give. The concept of data is for example used about that which is known in a calculation: it takes two men eight hours to dig a hole in the ground which is one cubic metre large. But data in qualitative inquiries are neither 'given' nor 'secure'. Nor are they 'collected', even though this is a common expression. On the contrary, it is evident in qualitative inquiries that the researcher plays an active and unavoidable role in the production of data. It would be possible to highlight this role by talking about *facts* instead, meaning that which has been done, from *facio*, I do, or about *capta*, that which has been taken, from *capio*, I capture, take or conquer. I have nevertheless retained the concept of data, to keep in line with common methodological discourse. Furthermore, when the research process and the active role of the researcher is viewed as a totality, there is still *something* which gives itself to the consciousness of the researcher, and which cannot be done or captured in an arbitrary way; and – after all – there can be epistemological gains for us by thinking about this something as *the given* or *data*.

What does it take for impressions, observations, perceptions, notes, and statements to become data? They somehow have to be ordered systematically. They have to contain principles, a system, 'an assemblage or combination of things or parts forming a complex or unitary whole'.[1] Based on such a system, it becomes reasonable to talk about certain data as 'given'. While retaining the open, explorative, and reflexive character of qualitative inquiries, I find it wise to pay a little more attention to the given nature of data (that is, of systematised data).

Displaying qualitative data

The word 'display' is even more conceptually complex than the word data. It has been chosen over other terms such as presenting and documenting, because of its multiple layers of meaning. The Oxford Advanced Learner's Dictionary (2000) contains no less than eight entries for the word 'display', four meanings of the word as a verb and four as a noun:

---

1 Webster's Encyclopedic Unabridged Dictionary of the English Language, Gramercy Books, New York. Revised edition, 1996.

1. (Verb) To put something in a place where people can see it easily, to show something to people
2. (Verb) To show signs of something, especially a quality or feeling
3. (Verb) To show information
4. (Verb) To show a special pattern of behaviour
5. (Noun) An arrangement of things in a public place to inform or entertain people or advertise something for sale
6. (Noun) An act of performing a skill or showing something happening, in order to entertain
7. (Noun) An occasion when you show a particular quality, feeling or ability by the way that you behave
8. (Noun) The words, pictures, etc. shown on a computer screen

The multiple layers of meaning, both in connection with showing, arranging, putting in place, and performing a description of something are all quite relevant in connection with the idea of displaying qualitative data. To show information is also to put it in a place where people can see it easily. The showing and performance of data is not easily separable. If the public arrangement is taken seriously, it will influence the performance. The way you perform your skill as a researcher has to be able to stand the test of public scrutiny.

Rules for displaying qualitative data

The word 'rule' comes from the Latin word *regula*, which means a straight piece of wood, i.e. a ruler. In its figurative sense, it means a guideline or rule.

In English, the word has six different meanings[2]: 1) it can refer to rules in a game, 2) in reference to advice in given situations, 3) in reference to habits or that which is normally true, 4) in reference systems (for example grammar), 5) it can refer to the rule of government in the sense of control, and 6) it can refer to the ruler as a measuring tool.

From the same Latin root, we derive the word 'regular', meaning normal, uniform, recurring, or orderly. At first sight, the idea of suggesting rules for the presentation (and production) of qualitative data seems incompatible with the open process and flexible design that characterises qualitative method. It may seem a step backwards to the old days when social scientific method was conceived of as *one* set of unalterable rules, whose mechanical application

---

2 According to Oxford Advanced Learners Dictionary (2000), Oxford University Press, Oxford. Sixth revised edition (first published in 1948).

to concrete inquiries was regarded as a more or less automatic guarantee for indisputable scientific quality.

However, this is not how I intend to use the concept of rules in this connection. Rules are not dogmas.

While the word 'dogma' refers to a prescribed doctrine,[3] the rule refers to a norm, i.e. a social construction or decision. A rule is constructed: in qualitative inquiries, it can be something one constructs or chooses to include, for example because it adds to the heuristic value or persuasive force of the inquiry. When displaying qualitative data, the rule has an additional excellent attribute: It can be used to give a concise explanation for how the researcher has treated a long series of data. This makes it possible for outsiders to see how data has been treated and presented.

It should be emphasised that the rule applies to 'a series of phenomena'. The rule may be irrelevant or invalid for phenomena falling outside of this category. It is often a question of interpretation to decide which phenomena should be covered by a rule, and in that case, which rule. The application of a rule may sometimes itself be subject to a rule; but it may also be a question of assessment. In either case, it would be an act of madness to imagine a comprehensive set of guidelines for the rules of rules within qualitative method. You reach a point where it is impossible (and in addition meaningless) to explicate everything. Therefore, it obviously takes both skill, competence, education, and apprenticeship – and an element of creativity – to become a good qualitative researcher. The methodology cannot and should not be turned into a set of thoroughly programmable actions.

In the words of Kvale (1996), the mechanical aspect of qualitative method cannot be reified and made independent; it has to be in constant dialogue with the cognitive aspect, i.e. the reflexive reasoning about concrete methodological steps.

But if a rule – although locally – has been applied with skill and reflection to a series of available data within an inquiry, it can lead to tremendous advantages.

A myriad of situational definitions and additional premises can be set up in connection with the local rule. But this does not detract from the usefulness of the local rule. Rules within qualitative method – even those of more local character – can have several far-reaching consequences, including consequences for the entire research undertaken. Relatively simple rules and rules that you (so far) agree on are preferable. So far.

---

3 Webster's Encyclopedic Unabridged Dictionary of the English Language, Gramercy Books, New York. Revised edition, 1996.

About rules in cooking

It is a good idea to add salt when you are boiling potatoes. But if you want to make mashed potatoes, it is better to leave the salt out. Whether these rules are of any relevance to you at all, depends on whether you are cooking today, whether you have potatoes or other types of grocery in the house, and whether you find yourself in a social and cultural situation where it would be appropriate to serve for example bangers and mash. But if you do, you should leave out the salt. Because otherwise the mash will get sticky. The rule is particularly suitable for persons who like mashed potatoes, but not sticky mash. Tastes differ. But the rule is still better than nothing, unless the people you are having over for dinner have declared that they prefer sticky mash.

CHAPTER 3
Displaying Data

> *Often, the young and inexperienced scientist will not be satisfied with limited questions...*
>
> Francois Jacob.[1]

> *Only in the tension between the somewhat shapeless reality and those restraints the artist puts on himself, is it possible to talk about true creativity.*
>
> Attributed to Oscar Wilde.

In this chapter I will suggest and exemplify some concrete rules for displaying qualitative data.

Taking stock

Let me begin with a short summary of the diagnosis. In chapter 1, I claimed that many qualitative inquiries suffer from a set of related weaknesses, namely that data and data treatment are given low priority and made invisible, and that the analysis solely is based on a more or less transparent selection of data, which in addition are unsaturated – i.e. they refer widely to different phenomena that are only loosely associated. In some cases, this situation is related to the fact that the entire process has been front-heavy. The researcher experiences that there is far too little time for the inquiry one had in mind, and almost all one's efforts are spent formulating the problem, reading the literature, designing the study, and accessing the field. Maybe the researcher is even left just before deadline with 1,000 pages of interview transcripts without knowing how to pull it all together and summarise it (Kvale, 1996).

Methodological reflections end with a deeply felt wish for more time; maybe

---

1 Jacob, 1985: 30. Author's translation.

Displaying Data

the researcher does not clearly see that it is possible to regard the timeframe as given, and instead ask exactly what it was that made the inquiry front-heavy within the given timeframe.

Figure 3.1 summarises this syndrome and provides a suggestion for what can be done about it.[2]

Figure 3.1

The syndrome	The result may be
• The research is front-heavy • Data becomes unsaturated • Data and data treatment are made invisible • Selected data is used to illustrate conclusions (exampling)	• The research work is more balanced • Data becomes saturated • Data and data treatment are more visible • Data supports conclusions
• One has to remain open • Structures and rules are always a Procrustean bed • Data is subjectively constructed • One has to reflect about the starting point, because it determines results	• One has to focus/bound data • Any interpretation is dependent on some degree of structure and rules • Data can be externalised • One has to work with data, because this work determines results

can often be attributed to these common notions ⟶ but if they are balanced by these ideas

'Common' notions of qualitative method are not downright wrong. Of course, one has to attempt to 'remain open' – it is the entire *raison d'être* of qualitative method that we should discover categories of which we were not previously aware. Of course, structure and rules for research may work as limitations,

---

2 This figure applies to typical front-heavy student reports based on qualitative inquiries. Qualitative consultancy reports with impressionistic conclusions and recommendations would require a somewhat different diagnosis, but they share the weak data analysis and they can also share the same medicine, as suggested in the following subchapters.

and they are often expressions of prejudices that keep the researcher from discovering new phenomena. Of course, we have to acknowledge that data springs from a subjective source; any observation is conceptually dependent and can be traced back to a long series of contextual, contingent conditions. Contingent means: it could have been different. Therefore, the researcher has to reflect about the observational situation, because it co-constitutes results. This last idea has been a major contributing factor to the remarkable cultivation of 'subjective starting points' in the discourse surrounding qualitative method. Thus, various –isms, such as e.g. feminism or gayism, in themselves almost seem to be arguments for taking a qualitative approach, just like the individual researcher's personal background and biography in some circles acquire an enormous, almost cult-like significance (Denzin and Lincoln, 2000, Schwandt 2006). The acclaimed strategies are confession and reflection, all in the name of subjectivism. Stories about qualitative inquiries often turn into 'confessional tales' (van Maanen, 1988), a kind of confessional literature where identity and authenticity are included as a guarantee for the quality of the qualitative insights.

The concept of data is almost forgotten or seems more or less old-fashioned and – using the ultimate insult – positivistic.

In order to balance notions of the kind described above, I put forward the following ideas:

It is, after all, necessary to focus and *bound* data. It is impossible remain open to everything all the time. It is necessary to define and delimit one's perspective to avoid ending up with a shapeless object of analysis.

To establish a perspective, it is necessary to apply some degree of rules and structure. It is true that the definition of perspective within a qualitative inquiry appears in conjunction with and as a function of the actual research work, but working entirely without delimitations is not feasible. Certain rules and structures have to define what is taken for granted, while focusing. Otherwise, it is *impossible* to focus.

Bounding is necessary to attain a certain degree of saturation of data. It is only when several data points start relating to the same phenomena that it is possible to draw conclusions.

In other words, it is only when the research process is delimited and boundaries are drawn that it opens itself up towards new conclusions based on its own premises. Establishing what is taken for granted and asking open questions are two sides of the same coin. Therefore, it is better to be conscious of *what* is taken for granted within the perspective, cf. Lars-Henrik Schmidt's idea of *active perspectivism* (Schmidt in Pedersen and Larsen, 1995, see also ch. 5).

Displaying Data   35

Game or play?

Sometimes children keep extending the framework when playing; they build another city; suddenly the Lego figures speak; then an Action Man enters the city, etc.

Sometimes children themselves try making up a game. Each participant has a castle, 24 knights, 2 messengers, and some land. They throw a dice, and within the constraints of 6 possible options dictated by the dice, they define which actions can be taken. It is a game as soon as the possible numbers of options are constrained, and certain rules and frameworks put limitations on which actions can be carried out. Probably, there is also a definition of how to win the game. Children can change the rules and invent a new game. But nevertheless, the game differs significantly from playing (in this example) by the fact that the game has a set of rules that define a limited set of options. The game is not funny if someone suddenly tilts another participant's knights without this being part of the rules.

In this sense, a qualitative inquiry resembles a game more than it resembles mere play. If it is to be interesting to inquire into the options, the options have to be limited.

Notice that the difference between playing and the game does not relate to who invented it. It is ok to invent your own game (just like it is ok for a qualitative inquiry to define its own perspective). But the game is not a game without a set of rules, structures, and frameworks defining the world of the game. Neither is it fun to take part in.

Any data created can be externalised. Granted, data is never entirely 'objective' and it is never an expression of 'God's eye view'. But data can be externalised to such an extent that it is possible to communicate effectively about it as data. It is central to scientific activity that it is based upon the value of shareability, and that knowledge thus can be subjected to public discussions (Bronowski, 1965) and that it can be repeated (Schmidt, 1991). Science aims for a de-subjectification of knowledge.

On the value of taking a second look: The Emperor's New Clothes

At a time when the word 'experience' is becoming obscure, it is obviously difficult to appeal to the concept of the empirical. The empirical means 'based on experience' – what you see when you inquire into something. Today, we see and experience much less unprejudiced and 'objectively' as scientific notions of yore almost made us believe. Nevertheless, empirical work still has its merits.

Once upon a time, there was an emperor who was infatuated with beautiful clothes. His infatuation was taken advantage of by two cunning fraudsters, who claimed to be tailors and, as we all know, made him a set of non-existing clothes. The emperor's most high-ranking officials were able to 'see' these clothes, because word had it that he who could not see it, was unfit for his office. When the emperor finally promenaded among his people, nobody dared admit that they were unable to see his clothes. Almost nobody, we should say. Because a little child was present, who was a really good empiricist. The child delimited what he was observing. And he clearly stated what he saw. 'He is not wearing anything'. The statement came from the only person to 'see' clearly. Among other things, this had to do with the fact that the child, unlike the other actors in the story, did not let his self-understanding interfere with the observation in a way that made his sight blurred or kept him from daring to say what he was actually observing.

Empirical observations are not infallible; the last few decades within philosophy of science tell one long tale of just *how* fallible they are. The American organisational researcher James March once (jokingly) said that you actually never ought to take on empirical investigations, because, as he says, *'You never know when you are right'*.

But simple and good empirical work is still an excellent source for challenging socially established conventions, which otherwise easily take out a patent on defining our shared reality – supported by power, hierarchy, the interests of officials, fraudsters, vanity, and fear of the consequence of seeing clearly and reporting what you see.

It is of great importance to insist upon the fact that the aim of science is to de-subjectify knowledge. This helps distinguishing scientific activity from other kinds of activity. The entire notion of defining qualitative research activity as a scientific activity will typically be rejected by adherents of subjectivism and 'cultivators of viewpoints', because it is practically impossible based on their own assumptions (Guba and Lincoln, 1989; Denzin and Lincoln, 2000).

It is an equally important notion that one has to work with data, because it helps constitute the results of the analysis. This notion seems so self-evident that few are ready to challenge it. But the recent discourse surrounding qualitative method has not gone in this direction; it has rather spent its efforts reflecting the *subjective starting points* of researchers (in terms of culture, institutions, history, politics, gender, ethnicity, biography, etc.)

One does not have to disregard these contingent factors to accept that data can make a difference. It actually does happen that data, and working with it, makes a set of notions tip. It also sometimes happens that the researcher creates data which is richer and more telling than you would expect, if you only kept to the starting point of the researcher.

One of the most beautiful examples of this is Linda Smircich's (1983) case study of an organisational culture entitled 'Organisations as Shared Meanings'. Her starting point is that organisations may be understood as a shared structure of meanings, which she wishes to illustrate via a case study. The case looks into a small group of leaders who do not at all share those structures of meaning that are central to the inquiry. This is obvious from data. But data does not make the researcher revise her conceptual focus on the *shared* meanings. The beauty of the study consists in the fact that even Smirchich's explicit prior understanding does not keep her from diligently and loyally reporting on the data she finds. Data is so clear that it actually manages to shine through the explicit and pedagogically posed prior understanding of the researcher.

You could argue that data per definition does not extend beyond the entire inner logic of an inquiry; Smirchich's research process as a whole has made her capable of 'seeing' data. But it does lie within the power of data to extend beyond what she as a researcher explicitly thinks is the logic and connection in her observations; in brief, it is possible for data to extend beyond the declared subjective starting point. And this suffices.

Put in another way, the perspective of an inquiry is not only constituted by the explicit and stated starting point of the researcher, but certainly also by the uncompromising integrity of the observations and the way in which one works with the data observations. This makes it interesting to suggest some rules that might be helpful when working with data.

Displays

A display is a table or other form of graphic presentation of qualitative data in a concentrated form. The display does not present a convenient selection of data or a particularly telling example. A display is constructed in a systematic manner. The display is constructed to present a complete set of data in one place, simultaneously facilitating an answer to a research question (Miles and Huberman, 1994: 188).

Displays and maps

To some extent, displays and maps are comparable. A map is based on a particular taxonomy. According to contemporary Western convention, cartography is based on the principle of representing a locality as seen from above and on a set scale (Kjelbo, 1966: 8). The reader is given a legend of how to read the signs on the map. Nor should the reader be left to himself when reading a display.

To a large extent, maps are based on conventions for representation; for example, North is usually at the top of the map. Displays are also based on certain conventions for representation. This means that even if displays may be perceived as objective, their design and the ways in which they are read is influenced by conventions.

Other examples of the common features of displays and maps will follow below.

In its simplest form, a display is a *list* of themes or phenomena that fall within a certain category. To produce such a list is a very important step to take when starting to analyse one's qualitative data. Doing this almost immediately raises a number of good questions. How can you be sure that a particular phenomenon should be included on the list? To answer this question, it is necessary first to thoroughly check one's definition of the category and once again compare it with every single phenomenon on the list. Once the list starts taking shape, what can be concluded about differences and commonalities between phenomena on the list? Do the commonalities give cause for a revision of the category, and do the differences give rise to new sub-categories?

In many cases, a list of observed phenomena within a category also gives cause – at a more general theoretical level – to ask whether those phenomena actually observed correspond with those phenomena it is conceptually possible to see within the framework of the category. Are there reasons for not having observed some of the possible phenomena in practice? How long might the list in principle be? When making lists of for example human needs, human emotions, or dimensions of the concept of quality, it makes a great theoretical difference whether these lists are regarded as in principle finite or infinite.

Displaying Data

Once a list has been more or less worked through, it is possible to cross it with another list of research themes, or with fundamental dimensions such as time, space, level of analysis, research unit, etc., and by doing so, you get a *matrix*.

Many displays are matrices (see e.g. Miles and Huberman, 1994). Displays can also be figures with squares and circles with key words connected by arrows. Displays can take on many different forms. But they often present variations of connections between a selection of basic research categories such as times, places, units, social relations, processes, etc.

Often a display in a qualitative research project can help overcome some of the problems with weak data analyses as discussed above. A display helps bounding data. Data becomes more saturated and close-knit. It communicates the content of the inquiry to the reader. The display can prevent situations of very intuitive readings of data. It explicates the bridge building from data to conclusion, because it presents all data on which the conclusion is based. Meanwhile, the display has also highlighted any possible gap or anomaly in the data set.

Of course, the display is not a miracle cure for every possible problem. It may not be used in all inquiries. It is not a mechanic quick fix to cure any flawed inquiry, irrespective of the content or insight aimed for. But a display can enhance the understanding of an issue both for the researcher and the reader, especially if one adheres to a few important rules. In the following, I will present three such rules and go on to show some practical examples of displays. There are great advantages to using these three rules when making displays, although I do not reject the possibility of designing displays that deviate from these. I simply wish to argue for – and proceed to demonstrate – some of the positive effects of these three rather simple rules.

The rule of authenticity

The first rule is *the rule of authenticity*. It says that as far as possible a display should present data in its original form. For example, interview transcripts should be applied directly, if available. Do not trust what you think you believe to remember was said! The rule of authenticity prevents consciousness from constructing recognisable impressions based on a very limited number of data – including false impressions. Without this rule, one might rashly construct an unrefined classification or prejudice; a whole organisation is rapidly diagnosed, and based on this, one 'understands' the situation within the entire research field.

The ability of human consciousness to construct totalities

At The Experimentarium in Copenhagen, one display shows three lines set at different angles. They are not set on the same plane, each protruding into space. However, when viewed from a particular demarcated spot, it looks as if the three lines form a perfect isosceles triangle. But your consciousness deceives you by producing an erroneous representation of reality based on a visual impression that provides a resemblance of a familiar object. Take one step to the side, and you will discover that the three lines never meet each other.

A little exercise

Peter's father has three sons. Their names are Tom, Dick and ... – what is the name of the third son? Many would be inclined to answer Harry, because this name fits a familiar pattern. But based on the available information ('authentic' data from the situation) we have already been presented with the fact that one of the sons is called Peter. So this is the correct answer to the question.

In this case, the rule of authenticity is a better guide than any spontaneously formed opinion about the matter.

Obviously, the rule of authenticity does not prevent all flaws. All data is representations of constructions and none are ultimately 'authentic'. But by returning to representations that lie prior to our summarised interpretations, we can sometimes force our consciousness to revise its conceptions.

Keeping to what you observe

The story goes that P. Munch (Danish minister and historian) once went for a car ride in Jutland. The chauffeur wants to keep the conversation going, and says, 'Look, the have sheared the sheep'. P. Munch lets the scientist in him answer with the words, 'Indeed, on the side we can see from here'. Bingo! The rule of authenticity applied.

Cartography and the rule of authenticity

The history of cartography contains numerous examples of maps representing pure conjecture. In some instances, guesses are based on travel experiences which have been given a wrong cartographic interpretation; sometimes because the experiences are added to maps which are flawed from the outset.

In 1576, British explorer Martin Frobisher travelled to the southern tip of Greenland; but because it had been placed much too northerly in an earlier map, he believed to have arrived at a separate island, 'Frisland'. This island had also appeared on a previous map, the so-called Zeno map, which reputedly was based on travels in the northern Atlantic by two Venetian brothers Antonio and Nicolo Zeno around the year 1380. It is still discussed within cartography whether the Zeno map is a downright forgery. It certainly contains a jumble of misplaced localities, probably distorted from several other maps.

In any case, the consequence was that subsequent to Frobisher's journey, a 'Frobisher-strait' was introduced between misplaced Greenland and the erroneously named land observed by Frobisher. This strait 'existed' until 1723, when Hans Egede on location established that there was no gap in the inland ice allowing for direct transport by ship between western and eastern Greenland (Kjelbo, 1966: 33)

The Portuguese cartographer Ribeiro (deceased in 1533) was probably one of the first clearly to leave costal lines open on his maps where no basis for further illustration was available. Maps and displays become more trustworthy if one abstains from filling in gaps with conjectures, instead leaving an obvious empty space where data does not cover.

Trap streets

Serious map makers sometimes face the problem that fraudsters relatively easily can copy their maps, erase the name of the copyright holder and sell the map in a slightly altered version. In this way, they can let other companies carry development expenses and dispense with copyright laws. To counter this dishonest practice, some map makers introduce so-called 'trap streets' in peripheral and insignificant localities, for example a dead end called 'Fido Lane' named after the cartographer's dog (Harvey, 2000). The purpose is to catch plagiarists in the act, when they unwittingly disclose themselves by reproducing a non-existent road which can have only one source. Trap streets are yet another good reason to obey the rule of authenticity!

Harvey (2000) is on the whole an entertaining book on the subject of cartographic crime!

The rule of inclusion

The second rule is the *rule of inclusion*. It says that all data falling within a particular category or delimitation (cell in the matrix) should be included in the relevant place within the display before drawing any conclusions. The display should not represent examples from a data set, but the data set in its entirety (Miles and Huberman, 1994) in relation to a particular category. While it is legitimate to select particular categories in the data set for presentation, all data falling within the given delimitation should be included in the display. The rule ensures that missing data, gaps, anomalies and deviations are also taken into consideration. This is because the rule dictates that the delimited portion of data under scrutiny has to be fully searched before conclusions are drawn. The results of qualitative analyses cannot always be generalised to cover time and space external to a particular inquiry. But internally, the conclusion has to apply to any data found during the inquiry (Alasuutari, 1995: 152).

Applying this rule can have the additional positive effect of making the researcher more skilled at explicating his or her field of study. Furthermore, the advantage of working with small – or at least clearly delimited – fields of study becomes evident. The idea of keeping an open mind can fruitfully be combined with the idea of keeping to a small field of study. Why? Because this makes it easier to apply the rule of inclusion.

What impact does the size of the field of study have?

Let S stand for the size of the field of study, in other words, the area in time and space one wishes to make assertions about. Let C stand for the degree of coverage, i.e. the number of phenomena per area unit one wishes to describe. Let E stand for the efficiency of the method, i.e. how good the method is in capturing the desired phenomena. Finally, let R stand for the amount of resources available to carry out the inquiry. Then the following connection holds good:

$S \times C = E \times R$

If for example one wishes to cover a large area using an inefficient method, it is necessary to have many resources at one's disposal. In case of limited resources, one has to opt for a very efficient method, a limited degree of coverage, and a small study field.

The history of charting and surveying Denmark through several attempts illustrates well how many resources it took, as long as the efficient method of aerial photography was not at our disposal. Thus, Jens Sørensen at the end of the 17th century used a homemade 'mile-barrow' with a bell attached. When this was pushed through the Danish landscape, the number of bell strokes helped keeping track of distances. But it took many journeys. In 1742, the Danish Scientific Society initiated an organised surveying of the entire country. The principle was based on using delimitation sticks to draw up north/south going parallel lines with 20,000 yards between them. The measurements were made using a 50 yard long steel wire. Subsequently, lines of sight based on characteristic objects along the entire line were drawn. To ensure that the work was actually carried through, farmers were ordered to put lodging, food, and drink at the disposal of the surveyors; and likewise, regional police officers were required to see to the maintenance of the delimitation sticks. During winter, topographical maps were assembled to form larger maps. In total, the surveying enterprise ended up taking approximately 80 years (Kjelbo, 1966: 65ff.). If one wishes to cover a large area thoroughly by using an inefficient method, it takes many resources.

Should the anomaly be included?

If twenty data points show one thing, and number twenty-one shows something different, is it legitimate to display only the first twenty? This was a question once raised by a student. The question is misdirected in two ways. First of all, the student asks permission from someone he or she believes capable of granting such permissions, while the real issue should be the researcher's own arguments for taking one approach or another. Secondly, number twenty-one is potentially just as loaded with information as the previous twenty data points taken together. The source of new knowledge lies in the deviation, the irritation, the disturbance. The contraction of several pieces of data is in itself an abstraction and to some extent an analysis. The role of the anomaly is exactly to make the contracted abstractions as potent as possible (see Alasuutari, 1995: 13 & 15). The anomaly has to be included to challenge the rest of the data. Hence the rule of inclusion.

In practice, there might not be room to include all data, but this problem is tackled by condensing and summarising data, for example by using key words or contracting sentences. How to condense meaning is further described by Kvale (1996: 193) and Alatuusari (1995: 7). Sometimes many data points can be represented by a single key word. Sometimes more are needed.

Condensing meaning is controversial because a statement may be condensed in several ways, dependent on one's perspective. But condensing meaning is actually often less controversial than many are led to believe. It is often possible to summarise the main points from a meeting and approve the minutes. This is related to the fact that we are well trained in condensing meaning. Methodologically, the condensation of meaning can be validated through a critical comparison of uncondensed and condensed statements (Kvale, 1996: 194), and in some cases through respondent validation (see chapter 4).

It should be noted that the rule of inclusion can be extremely costly in terms of resources if one keeps making new coding categories leading to new searches through data. In such instances, it is sometimes necessary to recode and condense meaning once again from the entire data set (to ensure that no relevant data has been excluded) and then proceed to rebuild the display.

In this way, the rule of inclusion becomes a practical counterweight to the temptation of continually coming up with new ideas, operating with a large field of study and/or repeatedly recoding data. New ideas and re-codings are certainly relevant and indispensable parts of qualitative method; but it is equally relevant and indispensable to point out that without some degree of steadiness in categories and codes (at least towards the end of an inquiry), it becomes

Displaying Data 45

impossible to obtain saturated data and consequently difficult to draw conclusions. These two considerations need to be weighed against each other. The rule of inclusion can help keep the balance.

> ### *The rule of inclusion and cartography*
>
> A map adheres to the rule of inclusion when the map actually represents all empirical phenomena within its area, corresponding with each item in the included legend. On a hiking map that includes signs for active volcanoes, one expects *all* active volcanoes in the area to be indicated on the map.

The rule of transparency

The third rule is the *rule of transparency*. This rule simply says that it should be transparent how the display has been designed. Its axes and dimensions should be well defined, and any possible problems with processing data should be openly tackled. A good set of rules for designing a display is recognisable by the fact that it is concise and brief. It is not a good sign if the processing of data comes across as random. If data is processed in different ways according to several different circumstances, which in themselves are complex and situational, the algorithm controlling the construction of the display can turn out to be more extensive than the entire data set. This is not a good sign either. Criteria for processing data should be parsimonious. Any explanation for these criteria should be relatively short in comparison with the amount of data. Only in this case, is the rule of transparency fulfilled.

> ### *Transparency and guidelines*
>
> Every good map includes a legend. When the rule of transparency is correctly applied, it is easy to see how individual phenomena within the display have been ordered, what they mean and how to understand them.

Below, I will give four different examples of how displays can be used in qualitative studies, all based on previous research. Readers are encouraged to discuss the examples and keep a sharp watch on whether the three rules mentioned are adhered to.

First example: Studying a strike at SAS[3]

After Jan Carlzon took over the role as manager of SAS, the company was often depicted as ideal with regard to its company culture. However, in 1989, two strikes occurred within the company. If the impression of an ideal company culture should have been maintained, these strikes ought not have occurred.

The first strike starts among cabin crew on 15 November after the SAS management in Stockholm announces a break away from previous principles of pan-Scandinavian seniority rankings for appointing pursers (team leaders among cabin crew). In the future, pursers are to be appointed according to which airport they typically fly from. The pan-Scandinavian principle means that occasionally pursers have to be flown from one airport to another before starting work. Therefore, costs can be cut by giving up this principle. Danish cabin crew are most senior and wish to maintain the principle.

The strike is called off as management promises to negotiate about the cause of the strike. However, the negotiations lead nowhere. Instead, a rumour breaks out among the cabin crew that the break-away from the pan-Scandinavian seniority principle is the first step in a larger strategic transferral of workplaces from Copenhagen to Stockholm. Nine days later, on 24 November, a new strike begins, this time with support from several groups of employees. A declaration of dissatisfaction with management's 'broken promises' of negotiation is issued. Following several hours of total mayhem at the airport, management declares loyalty towards the pan-Scandinavian seniority principle and work is resumed.

I ask the following questions: How did the strikes make sense? Within which cultural universe were employees able to join these strikes? And what had happened to the so-called excellent company culture in this universe of meanings? Had it been transformed or forgotten, or had the ideal impression of the company culture been misleading from the outset?

To begin with, I decide to focus intensely on the interpretation of the strike by the small group of employees who took the initiative to start it all. I assume they are able to give explicit reasons for the strike. Another, bigger – and possibly less important – job would lie in finding out how many of the strikers shared these interpretations. With this choice, my claim is considerably narrowed down. Later, this will turn out to strengthen the inquiry, or at least make it more defensible.

I am allowed a four-hour group interview with the organising committee behind the strike. Prior to this, I research the history of the strike and the

---

3 For a more comprehensive illustration of this inquiry, see Dahler-Larsen (1993) and Dahler-Larsen (1997).

company via news, articles, and consultancy reports. The interview is loosely structured – above all, I am interested in their own conception of the history and background of the strike. I ask follow-up questions as we go along. I am particularly interested in the typification of 'we' among the strikers. This is because I know that all cultures create a feeling of who 'we' are; and when a strike occurs against 'your own' company, it is interesting to follow how the 'we' is delimited – as it later turned out, there were several typifications of 'we'. I also interview other people, a union representative and some ordinary members of cabin crew. I collect folders distributed during the strike.

Then I approach the transcript of the long group interview. I start by coding the statements. The work is made easier by the fact that I am looking for typifications of 'we'. These are linguistic expressions directly visible within sentences. It turns out that there are four different types of 'we' within the material: we as cabin crew, we as members of SAS, we as employees, and we as Danes. These types had not been identified prior to collecting the data.

Encouraged by the fact that there seems to be substance in the idea of looking at the typifications of 'we', I ponder over ways in which they can be further described. Having returned to cultural theory, I operate with the following three ways of characterising a 'we'.

a. What are the central values for the we? Presumably, a collective holds something sacred (Durkheim according to Nisbet, 1966) which helps constitute and maintain a sense of community and create a 'consciousness of kind' (van Maanen and Barley, 1984), a consciousness of unity.
b. Who are 'they' as opposed to 'we'? A basic premiss for the definition of 'we' is often a contradistinction to others, a 'consciousness of difference' (van Maanen and Barley, 1984).
c. What is the relationship between 'us' and 'them', i.e. how is the border regulated between 'we' and 'them', between insiders and outsiders? In cultural theory, any such borderline is filled with significance.

Structurally, these three characteristics for each of the four typifications of 'we' can be displayed as an empty 4x3 matrix.

I then reread the interview and code in more detail, so that data belonging to each cell in the matrix is given each its own code. I distribute all the statements in the cells and sum up the content of each cell using one or a few meaning condensing key words. I am encouraged by the fact that statements within individual cells are redundant (i.e. repeat the same information) and by the fact that there are no empty cells.

I now return to my interviewees for respondent validation. Both orally and in writing I go through the matrix and explain how the key words are connected to their statements and discuss whether the matrix gives a fair summary of their viewpoints.

This leads me to correct one key word which was unnecessarily complicated, and I regard the matrix as accepted by the respondents. It looks like this:

Figure 3.2 Typifications of "we" by the organising committee

	We as cabin crew	We as members of SAS	We as employees	We as Danes
Most important value	Service	SAS experience	Respect	Non-authoritarian
Who are 'they'?	Other employees	New employees	Management	Swedes
Relation	Contributing to functionality	Socialisation	Negotiation	Autonomy

I support my presentation of key words within the display with explanatory quotes. I describe each we in turn. Cabin crew takes pride in being able to deliver good service. No other group of employees makes an equally important contribution to the relationship between everybody within the company. As members of SAS, employees have a long-standing experience with the company and its values, as opposed to new employees who need to be socialised first. Employees demand respect; management should handle issues via negotiation rather than dictation. Danes uphold anti-authoritarian values and wish for autonomy in relation to the more authoritarian Swedes, who unfortunately harbour the SAS headquarters.

The matrix is checked against data from other interviews (with respondents outside the organising committee) and no discrepancies are encountered.

Based on the matrix, the strike can be explained. Especially columns number one and two are mobilised in connection with the first strike. The termination of the pan-Scandinavian principle of seniority is both an affront to the SAS experience reached precisely via seniority, and a disregard for service delivery by cabin crew as a significant contribution to the joint working of the entire company. Luckily, the strike demonstrates that without cabin crew it is impossible to fly.

During the second strike, columns three and four are also mobilised. The conflict between management and employees flares up because of management's 'broken promise', which vexes other groups of employees besides cabin crew. The Danish/Swedish conflict is mobilised by rumours about transferral of jobs to Stockholm, and by the decidedly 'Swedish' (i.e. authoritarian) way the conflict is handled.

The typifications of 'we' are presented so that cabin crew, employees, SAS members, and Danes are on the same side against other groups of employees, management, new employees, or Swedes. In brief, the recently employed, business school trained managers at the Swedish headquarters are categorised as *being outside company culture*. On the basis of these classifications, it becomes possible to strike *in support of* a company culture experienced as one's own. It is the company culture of the striking employees too, because they integrate some of the familiar themes about service and company loyalty in their own account and interpretation of the situation.

When reporting my findings to research colleagues, I try to relate the four we-definitions to already existing cultural theory. It comes as no surprise that I find these four, because theories on organisational culture often focus on describing functional groups, management versus employees, company culture, and national differences. Often, these four cultural configurations are analysed separately, because any study of them typically is segmented in different types of literature and different research fields; but my case exemplifies the dynamics and interplay between them.

I am asked whether I have missed a gender dimension within my data, a possible fifth 'we' distinguishing between women versus men. I recheck my material, but do not encounter this distinction. I explain this by the fact that both women and men are present within the organising committee, the spokesperson is a man and most cabin crew are women, so it seems only logical that any potential gender conflict is not mobilized in this particular situation.

A few notes about the display from this example: It is only possibly for me to procure sufficiently saturated data for the display because I limit data collection to the organising committee. It would be the straight road to boundless data collection to aim to draw conclusions about all 1200 striking employees. In addition, it would not be particularly interesting. Focus in this intensive qualitative inquiry is concentrated on the substance of the significations, not their extension.

The display is designed relatively early during the inquiry, more or less half way through. The display is based on a juncture of theoretical ideas and concrete data. Already during the interview, I ask clarifying questions about the typifications of 'we', but it is data which decides which typifications appear. Closer characterisation of the typifications of 'we' is theoretically inspired. But it only survives because it is tested against data. If the 4x3 matrix could not be filled in in a sensible way, this idea would not have been upheld.

The display is thus validated in several ways, both via respondent validation, via communication with other researchers, and I also investigate whether I have missed a dimension, etc.

Second example: Organisational structures within Bordurian agriculture

In 1994, a Western donor organisation wanted to support a privatisation process within agriculture in former Warsaw bloc country Borduria[4] – one of Europe's poorest countries. In practice, the project was envisaged to extend loans towards the acquisition of agricultural machinery. I partook in a team of consultants who were to undertake a pilot investigation paving the way for a possible project. My particular role was to research organisational structures. The utility of supporting acquisition of machinery depends on how the machines are owned, distributed, and used. Consequently, an understanding of organisational structures is essential to the project. But this is not an easy assignment; the organisational structures undergo rapid changes, as old large state-owned farms fade into history and a new structure has not yet stabilised.

It is part of the context that privatisation of land (as well as other former state-owned goods) in former East bloc countries have occurred in two fundamentally different ways. In Estonia, land has been distributed according to whom could document ownership on a given date prior to World War II. In this way, large connected areas of land have been given to persons who often have no affiliation with agriculture, or to deceased persons whose heirs might not be particularly interested. In Borduria, formerly state-owned farm land is divided by the number of employees, which results in each person getting approximately 3.5 acres. By any measure, this is too little for modern rational farming methods. It is also too little for each farmer to be able to make good use of a reasonable assembly of machinery. On the other hand, it is a good principle, because everybody can have a piece of land, and because only the present generation of farmers are given some land.

It is possible to compensate for some of the disadvantages of each of the two principles for privatisation by making it possible to buy and sell land. This is not done in Borduria. Possibly to safeguard various interests from being overrun by capitalist money makers, the law prohibits any trade in agricultural land.

Although I had studied the history and present situation of the country

---

4   The name of the country is fictional. It has been borrowed from the Tintin cartoon 'King Ottocar's Sceptre'.

before arrival (and previously had partaken on a comparable assignment in a different country), there was a lot I did not know about the field I was about to research. Most available material was rapidly outdated by present profound changes.

Working conditions amounted to: a good driver, an old Lada bearing a sign with the inscription 'Hüte dich vor blonde Frauen und Autos die Russen bauen'[5], a good interpreter from a local liaison office, a notebook, a laptop, good teamwork, and approximately one week in the field.

I ask myself a few initial working questions, such as

- Which factors excert an influence on the choice of organisational structures?, e.g.
- Which connections exist between machinery and organisational structures?
- Is the Western model of farms with individual owners the right model for Borduria?

During field work I attempted to structure the answers to these questions, but was overwhelmed by the many contingencies which turned out to be of relevance: crop, cultivation methods, political forces impacting on agricultural laws, laws concerning organisational structures, economy, and agricultural accountancy. In addition to all this came impressions from a lot of actual localities, particular persons, and concrete stories. It also became clear that a number of formerly state-owned farms were carried on in different legal forms as so-called 'joint stock companies' (locally referred to as jsc's) with more or less unaltered operation and management. Here, employees remained wage earners rather than co-owners.

I visited many different kinds of farms all over the country. I spoke with farmers about their lives. This often took place in the fields. I asked rather open-ended questions about their lives, crops, their problems and hopes for the future, about their machinery and possible cooperation with others. Many different forms of cooperation existed.

I put down as detailed notes as possible from each location, and in the evening I typed them up on my laptop to gather my thoughts. But I was becoming increasingly worried about how to synthesise the material. While working on the material, I was struck by the high degree of instability of organisational forms described in the case stories.

At one stage, I started to cross-examine the stories to look for arguments by farmers in support of the organisational structure they were presently working

---

5 Beware of blonde women and cars built by Russians.

under, or the structure they wished to change into. Most of the case stories contained such arguments, as organisational structures seemed to be under continual change. For example, many farmers wished to gain autonomy and influence, and therefore wanted smaller units. Many farmers wanted to leave the large old collectives where they were still working. This was an option within the legal framework, and when doing so they would obtain the previously mentioned 3.5 acres as well as a proportional share of buildings and machinery. Even when several people left jointly, this turned out to be an extremely difficult step to take. All manner of formal and practical obstacles appeared. In some cases, the managers of the collectives openly attempted to obstruct the process, in other cases there was nothing much in working condition to be shared.

The lack of machinery thus appeared to be a considerable obstacle to the privatisation process. Simultaneously, there were self-evident arguments against an atomisation of organisational structures into individually owned farms. Wishes for access to machinery and the ability to share farming land in order to practice crop rotation to avoid soil exhaustion counted in favour of joining smaller shares, or at least working closely together. It is important to keep in mind that the 3.5 acres per person functioned as a historic institutional limitation, and that in a country like Borduria few alternatives to farming exist. Consequently, an isolated argument about efficiency – few people, plenty of land – does not apply to the situation.

I envisaged a comprehensive picture of the situation where the various dynamics impacting on the choice of organisational structures would be evident.

To organise this picture, I found it useful to divide all the case stories into various main types. Maybe this would enable me to see the dynamics as arrows pointing from one main type to another.

Four different main types of structures became evident during this process:

1. Old collectives carried on as joint stock companies.
2. Large associations involving many farmers, having an elected leadership and not necessarily involving close personal acquaintance. These had generally come into being via a jointly organised emigration from a collective.
3. Smaller associations (typically 2-8 persons who knew each other well) sharing machinery and cultivation.
4. Individually owned farms.

I then made a display of organisational structures with each arrow representing an argument to turn from one organisational form to another. I included

Displaying Data

arguments both for forms already chosen and for forms wished for. I included potential changes on purpose, to get as broad a material as possible. I read the descriptions diligently and included all arguments. If one argument was repeated several times, I only let it count as one arrow for the sake of clarity. I checked the arguments in my notebook. The result was the following display.

Display: Dynamics impacting on the choice of organisational forms:

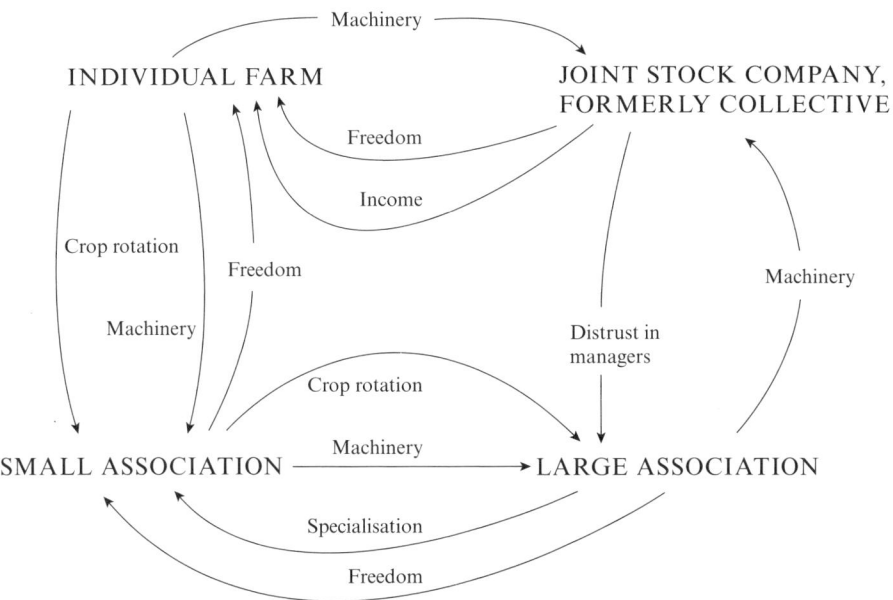

I found that the display gave a good holistic impression of the opposing forces impacting on the dynamics of organisational forms. The argument about freedom in each instance pointed towards smaller organisational forms. But the need for crop rotation also had an impact, and appeared to favour smaller associations, as opposed to individually owned farms. The argument about access to machinery each time pointed towards larger organisational units. Thus, the lack of machinery can easily become a substantial obstacle to developing alternatives to the former collectives. The control of machinery risks becoming a strategic factor used by people wanting to maintain the dominance of the large collectives.

Looking at the display it is in no way evident that individually owned farms should be a particularly good solution – even if we are prone to support models we are familiar with when giving aid to other countries. Instead, larger and smaller associations appear equally efficient if a compromise between various needs is sought: on one hand, needs springing from large scale benefits such as the use of machinery and crop rotation, and on the other hand, the freedom and democratic influence of individual farmers. It would even be possible to image smaller associations within larger ones to allow for particular needs for specialisation.

The display ended up approximately half-way through the chapter about organisational structures within the report. In the second half of the chapter, I went more into depth in differentiating the various organisational forms, both with regard to specific legal frameworks existing in Borduria and with regard to experiences from other countries concerning the organisation of small and large associations (looking both at cultivation, management, economy, democratic influence, etc.).

Third example: How shop stewards use the word 'democracy'.

In 1999, the Danish trade union TU[6] was planning an entirely new educational program for shop stewards and security stewards, and in planning this, TU was interested in knowing what issues these representatives at Danish work places were tackling on a daily basis.

The union harboured a number of ideas concerning content and form for this new educational concept. Among other ideas was the notion that the joint headline for the program ought to be 'democracy', based on the consideration that democracy is about involving people in changes affecting their lives. Therefore, the joint assignment for both shop and security stewards is essentially a question of democracy.

I arrange with the union to carry out an inquiry into how shop stewards view their role in relation to processes of change at a number of selected Danish companies.

I visit just over twenty, mostly at their workplace. I ask a number of open-ended questions about the nature of their work, about changes, colleagues and management, and about easy and difficult aspects of being a shop steward. Among other things, I ask about how they find their bearings and which values they adhere to as shop and security stewards. Concretely, I for example ask about which goals it is important to reach, which interests have to be included, and what cannot be left on the line – typically in relation to one or the other conflict or change experienced at the workplace. Typical answers include, 'the health and safety of employees', 'continued employment', 'wage increases', 'that

---

6   The name of the union is fictional.

Displaying Data 55

we are treated with respect by management,' etc. The concept of democracy is notable by its absence.

Having completed the round of interviews I decide to make a display collecting all the spontaneous statements by shop stewards about the concept of democracy. This results in the following display:

Display: Spontaneous statements by shop and security stewards about the concept of democracy:

The display is empty. It shows that the word 'democracy' is not part of the ordinary vocabulary of interviewees when discussing values and interests impacting on their every day role at workplaces. Obviously, this does not imply that democratic values are irrelevant. Quite possibly, interviewees express such values in alternative ways. But if a completely new educational program is to be promoted under the headline 'democracy' to a target group, it is essential to know what significance this concept carries within the vocabulary of the said target group. Therefore, this display brings home a message.

Representing results to the union, I supplement this display with another one containing statements by shop stewards in response to my more direct and explicit questions about the concept of democracy in relation to their work. I thus produce two different displays. The first one (represented above) is based on spontaneous statements by shop stewards based on their active vocabulary, the second one shows their answers after having been directly asked by me about the concept of democracy. I argue that it makes a difference whether a concept is part of the active vocabulary of a target group or not.

I also touch upon responses to training programs for shop and security stewards, changes in these programs, and the suitability of different possible headlines for the new educational program. I also present a closer examination of the involvement of shop stewards in various processes of change within the workplaces; so the empty display is not the only finding I present.

Advice on making displays[7]

Based already on the research question and the most important variables or phenomena within it you should be able to make a rough sketch of your display.

Get feedback from a colleague about your ideas for a display. Discuss any assumptions you make as well as alternative modes of representation.

Design the display so that it will fit on one sheet of paper – if necessary, a large sheet attached on the wall. You need to be able to get an overview of the entire display in one look.

Do not attempt to introduce more than a dozen variables or phenomena in rows and columns. Otherwise you will have to join them together in 'streams' or 'families', or divide the display into more parts.

Be ready to re-design the display as you go along, for example by
- Adding, deleting, or moving rows and columns
- Dividing a display
- Joining more displays into one

Strike a balance in the level of detail: sufficiently detailed to distinguish between qualitatively different phenomena, but also sufficiently aloof not to be lost in inconsequential detail.

Fourth example: General practitioners' use of a new preventive treatment

A student wishes to inquire how and why GPs introduce a new preventive treatment, so-called 'preventive consultations', which are structured dialogues between a patient and a member of the health personnel in order to motivate the patient to engage in health-promoting behaviour. The problem is generally relevant both in relation to preventive treatment as such, and in relation to questions about how the work of GPs is controlled and changed by health authorities.

The new treatment is based on conversations with patients, which presupposes both a renewal of the relation between patient and health workers, as well as, in many cases, a renewal of relations between various groups of health workers at the clinics. This new concept fits more or less well into an institutionalised pattern of relations in the health sector generally, and in individual clinics.

---

[7] Based on Miles and Hubermann, 1994: 241.

The Ph.D.-student carries out qualitative studies at 10 clinics, reads the literature and formulates a wide set of hypotheses about which factors may influence the implementation and elaboration of the new concept. Every possible aspect is included, ranging from attitudes towards preventive treatment, accountancy systems, communication at the clinic, paper work routines, the relationship between groups of employees, relations between doctors and patients, physical organisation, etc. She sends elaborate case reports back to each clinic to check the validity of her observations. But systematic analysis is still not in sight.

The student experiences a break-through in the development of the research project at the time of making a display with the following main structure.

Display: Factors that influence how the clinics make use of the new type of preventive conversation

	Input I1 I2 I3 I4 I5...	Process P1 P2 P3 P4....	Result R1 R2 R3...
Clinic 1			
Clinic 2			

Clinic 10			

The numbers in the display under respectively input, process, and result refer to various qualitative aspects relating to each of these headlines. This might for example be 'attitude towards preventive treatment at the clinic', 'suitable room for carrying out preventive consultations', 'appointment calendar', 'does the clinic register effects of consultations', 'the GP's notion of whether other employees are qualified to carry out the consultation', 'who carries out the consultation', 'the thematic focus of the consultation,' etc.

The basic structure of the display comes as no surprise for anyone used to thinking systematically about data matrices, including quantitative data matrices. But the display came into being in an entirely different way than merely by schematically making a list of variables, because in this case, the display is based on a substantial amount of field work.

The display immediately fosters a number of good questions: Does the field work that has already been carried out in the clinics adequately supply data to systematically fill in all cells in the display? Are case reports from each of the clinics fully represented – i.e. is the condensing of meaning acceptable – if each clinic is described by one row in the display?

How is the fit between more exact definitions of issues I1-I5, etc., and those data which are subsequently filled into the cells in each column? And last but not least: Is there cause for a revision of the way in which the 'use of preventive consultations' is described both conceptually and in terms of data? How the clinics use the concept may be described both as an adoption versus non-adoption and as different individual variations in the actual implementation among the adopters. Last but not least, the display makes it possible to start building explanations of the differences between the clinics. The display opens the possibility of moving stepwise from an in-depth qualitative description of each clinic towards a more comparative explanatory strategy. The comparative approach still allows for qualitative combinations of factors to play an explanatory role (Ragin 1994), rather than isolated variables known from purely quantitative strategies.

Even if a substantial amount of work still needs to be carried out, the display looks promising. It provides an overview of the structure of data. It displays what still needs to be done. And it points to a number of interesting analytic possibilities, both for understanding of how the individual clinics use the concept on the basis of a combination of factors, and for cross-referencing some of these factors with each other in future displays.

Summing up on the displays

The four displays shown in connection with the above examples all take on different *shapes*. We have a list (an empty one) in the third display, we have lists combined into matrices in number one and four, and a graphic depiction of words and arrows in the second one.

In addition, all four displays contain a number of *concepts* which serve as bridgeheads between theoretical ideas and empirical observations. In the first display the bridgehead consists in the concept of typifications of 'we' and the three ways in which they can be characterised. In the second display, the bridgehead consists in arguments in favour of changing organisational structures. In the third display, it is the word 'democracy'. The fourth describes a 'process'. By 'bridgehead' I mean to imply a phenomenon comparable to indicators knows from quantitative methods. An indicator serves as an operationalization of a theoretical concept. An indicator indicates what one should look for empirically to see a theoretical concept played out in practice.

Bridgeheads (like indicators) point towards more abstract conceptualisations. Typifications of we are indicators of feelings of cultural community; arguments in favour of changing organisational structures point towards the dynamics at play within a system of organisations; statements about the word 'democracy' indicate the status of this term in the conceptual universe of the stakeholders. Aspects of inputs, processes and results are ways of characterizing theoretically relevant ways in which the clinics deal with the new preventive consultations.

But while it is important that bridgeheads point towards theoretical assumptions, it is equally important that they are also readily applicable on empirical phenomena. In the examples above, bridgeheads have generally been chosen among concepts that are directly expressed and readily linguistically recognisable in interview statements and/or documents. Many students make life hard on themselves by operating with very abstract research categories without corresponding concrete bridgeheads when doing qualitative analyses. Instead, I aim to ensure a close connection between bridgeheads and raw data material.

The number of research units vary. In the example from SAS, the display is based on one (long) group interview. In the other examples, approximately 20 units (respectively 20 farms or 20 shop and security stewards) or ten clinics are summarised in one display.

The amount of content varies as well. An empty display can be used in a presentation, if the emptiness carries significance. But an empty display is obviously only interesting if the rule of inclusion has been adhered to! This is another good reason to stick to this rule: sometimes it becomes possible to draw up some really telling empty displays.

The four displays were designed at *different stages during the research process*. In the example from SAS, the basic structure of the display was developed comparatively early on in the process. In the example from Borduria, the display was designed worryingly late in the process. Some researchers (Padilla, 1994) recommend drawing up an empty display already when starting an inquiry, as a help in structuring the data collection process. All one has to do, then, is fill in the display. This approach is not consistent with a lot of basic wisdom within qualitative method, where researchers are encouraged to be as open as possible, to study the field without any preconceptions and let ones codes be grounded in field observations (Glaser and Strauss, 1967). It can, however, be acceptable, productive, and in accordance with the purpose of qualitative methodology to draw up an empty display in advance – provided one is prepared to adjust the structure of the display and its axes (and not just content within cells) as a result of the inquiry. An important point in qualitative method is that research categories are up for flexible testing and development. *Come to that, there is nothing illogical about listing analytic categories in advance and subsequently revising them on the basis of research data.* On the contrary, it becomes more obvious what needs to be revised if one works with explicit preliminary categories. It is harder to revise analytic categories that have not been explicitly formulated.

In this way, it can be both productive and commendable to operate with explicit empty displays at an early stage during an inquiry. Their relevance obviously has to be tested against data. Revising the structure of a display can be an important outcome of an inquiry.

Do not forget the anomalies!

Some displays turn out to be so comprehensive that it becomes impossible to procure all the necessary data within an inquiry of reasonable duration and volume. In such cases, the displays have to be adjusted. Discovering the size of a field of study and finding out how to conceptually delimit it can be a valuable lesson to learn.

In some cases, data is missing for a particular cell within a display. If the display as a whole makes sense, an empty cell quite often is theoretically reasonable. However, before looking for a theoretical explanation, it is necessary to ask oneself whether there are methodological reasons for the gap in the display – and, if so, one has to make changes in the methodological design to ameliorate this.

One of the most important functions for a display is to identify anomalies (atypical data in relation to expectations, categories, etc.). However, anomalies are only brought out if the research categories have been sufficiently explicated. An important function for displays is to further such an explication. Following this, the anomaly serves to illustrate the limits of the given research categories. It is the disturbance, the crisis, the anomaly which bring out the essence of the categories, highlights their limitations and points to any possible directions in which they need to be developed. Highlighting the limitations of the categories can in itself be a valuable epistemological task. A concrete sign of the presence of an anomaly is that one might have to revise the definition of columns or rows to fit a particular piece of data into the display – or one might have to design an entirely new display.

Concerning atypical cases

'I wish to be listed under 'miscellaneous' in the history books, because I don't fit anywhere else'

Paraphrase from Staceyann Chin

Displaying Data

Asymmetrical displays

Sometimes displays turn out asymmetrical. Sometimes researchers subconsciously work with an asymmetrical display, failing to draw it up. Asymmetrical displays describe one set of characteristics pertaining to a research unit, and other characteristics pertaining to other units. Asymmetrical displays often indicate that data is missing and/or that the theory construction is not sufficiently integrated or close-knit. Such asymmetrical structures often remain hidden within written presentations. If a graphic presentation is essayed, the dissymmetry becomes more obvious. In such cases, one is urged to search for the missing data and develop a theoretical explanation.

Asymmetrical displays – an example

A researcher explains the impetus for collaboration between organisation A and organisation B by the fact that A stands to gain financially, while B views the collaboration as a source of symbolic legitimation. Thus, the available data supports the following graphic display.

	Organisation A	Organisation B
Financial advantages	X	
Symbolic advantages		X

This display is evidently asymmetrical. The explanatory power of the theory might be strengthened if it were possible to include any financial advantages for organisation B and any symbolic advantages for organisation A. It might be argued that there are theoretical explanations for the two organisations to be driven by different impetuses, etc. One might also bring both kinds of *disadvantages* into consideration, for example by splitting each row into a positive and a negative side. In any case, an asymmetrical display should serve as an analytic warning signal. Something needs to be done.

An asymmetrical display can be regarded as a more or less conscious attempt to weasel out of possible anomalies. It is certainly worth considering whether the theoretical explanation might change if the display is straightened out.

Drawing conclusions from displays

A display often brings different data on the same phenomenon together. The displays *works* when data starts indicating a coherent set of dynamics within a process or system. This is *inference* – i.e. that patterns spring from the data set as whole and not simply from the sum of the parts. Inference is the process of using the facts we know to learn facts we do not know (King, Keohane and Verba, 1994: 46). Inference means to draw conclusions on the basis of visible facts within a display to conceptual relationships which are not immediately visible. Often (but not always) this involves a process of developing a concept to describe a synthesis between the joint data.

A common *pattern* might be immediately obvious. But inference can also appear through disparities within data, which can be resolved and overcome when they are *integrated into a larger common explanation.*

> ### *A simple example of inference.*
> Some employees within an organisation react by retracting their personal involvement in the organisation, while others display strong emotional reactions at the workplace. The concept of stress might explain both patterns of reactions. It becomes possible to conclude on the phenomenon of stress in itself when viewing these two patterns of reactions as part of the same conceptual formation.

In some cases, conclusions are based on data within the display. In other cases, the phenomenon of inference impacts on the division of categories within the display. In such cases, it is necessary to redesign the display.

In both cases, the process of explicating the display can in itself be the redeeming factor which carries a qualitative inquiry substantially further.

> ### *Idea for new analysis*
> The Ph.D.-student from example four above discovered that the clinics used different ways of documenting the effects of consultations. This calls for a more subtle understanding of the process of implementing the new consultations at the clinics, because this means that it may take the shape of a prolonged learning process with feed-back loops, and not simply resemble a linear input-process-result model, which the display in example four otherwise suggests.

The observation that some clinics themselves document results of the consultations provides the possibility for drawing up a display with four cells, wherein the implementation of the new treatment (Yes/No) is cross-tabulated with an internal documentation system (Yes/No). This provides interesting analytic possibilities, among other things because the ideal within a large segment of the medical field is that new initiatives should be based on evidence, which in this connection usually means 'confirmed by randomised, controlled experiments'. If some clinics – entirely in line with the spirit of the times – cultivate their own systematic practice for ensuring quality, this simply provides more than one answer to what is systematically effective.

How a display fits into the research process

A successful display is more or less self-explanatory. But the shape and content of a display cannot be understood in isolation from the inquiry of which it is a part. A display is simply one out of several parts of the presentation which describes an inquiry. A display needs to harmonise with the entire analytic text within a report (Miles and Hubermann, 1994), and a display needs to be related to the entire set of written texts describing an inquiry (notes, memos, drafts, etc.). The validity of data in a display does not pertain to the display itself, but rather to the many mutually dependent choices made during the process of inquiry as a whole. I shall return to this point in the following chapter on quality criteria within qualitative inquiries.

Qualitative researchers are often prone to regard their data (and their displays) as being unable to speak for themselves. This contributes to the difficulty of joint filings of qualitative data (See Anne Sofie Fink (2000) for an excellent discussion).

When qualitative researchers tell about their data, they have a tendency to draw in so much contextual information that a distinction between text and context is blurred. A display is an excellent way to narrow down focus, while circumstantial information about the inquiry precisely is delegated to the surroundings. The display is text, the rest is context. This is a healthy set of priorities to stick to. It helps the researcher focus the inquiry. And it helps prioritising the often limited time available to communicate results to others. Innumerable qualitative researchers have spent their sparse time at conferences accounting for the background for their inquiry (a front-heavy presentation), running out of time before approaching anything resembling their key findings. Therefore, it is a healthy exercise for the qualitative researcher to design a display which is as self-explanatory as possible. *In the final instance, the scientific quality of an inquiry hinges on its shareability, i.e. that it is possible to present results in a relatively de-subjectified discussion among peers.* One might spoil this by being unable to limit the amount of contextual information about the data before presenting it.

However, it is obvious that a display cannot stand totally alone in relation to the context of the inquiry it springs from. Below, I will briefly sketch some of the contingencies within an inquiry which impact on the conditions for producing a given display. Often, it will be reasonable to account for these conditions in the text surrounding a display, not least within a report's methodological chapter. The following comments will be short, as many of these problems already are well covered by existing literature on qualitative method – see the references.

Negotiating the birth and design of an inquiry

Qualitative inquiries are social interactions that are dependent on other social interactions. Often, it is a question of negotiation whether an inquiry will in fact be carried out (Mirvis, 1985).

Researchers are driven by motives, and organisations have gatekeepers (Hammersley and Atkinson, 1987) deciding whether a researcher will be given access, dependent on his errand, reputation, and standing. Another decisive factor can be how the organisation sees its own advantages and disadvantages in relation to an inquiry, including whether they find the research question interesting (Maaløe, 1996: 140 ff.), what they perceive the researcher might contribute to the organisation, how they estimate the consequences of any publicity about results etc. Often, persistent and opposing interests will be present in such relations. While an organisation wishes to maintain its organisational culture as something sacred, the researcher wishes to make it profane.

A delicate question relating to this is whether the researcher him/herself operates with an overt or a covert research agenda. Even if the researcher believes to have clearly presented his/her approach, for example 'an analysis of organisational culture', members of the organisation might not understand this in the same way as the researcher, and they might see more or fewer implications of such an approach than the researcher him/herself. It is the organisation's own conceptions which determine its way of relating to the inquiry. A clear and explicit research contract is good to have, but such a contract, like any other contract between human beings, will carry with it a number of implicit assumptions, and it might be necessary to operate under a double entry (Mirvis: 1985). Winsløw (1991: 21) claims that the informant will often be fundamentally unable to understand the purpose of a qualitative inquiry because of the frequently great distance between the relevance structure of scientific researchers and the life-world of the informant. Consequently, the informant will relate to the researcher on the basis of his/her own ideas, not on the basis of the ideas of the researcher. This often impacts on an inquiry, even if the researcher may not be able to see it, and even if the researcher believes to have clearly stated his/her purpose.

Organisational interests and inquiries

During the 80s, it was SAS's stated interest in connection with the use of inquiries into the company to 'document changes and create positive attention' (Edström, Norbäck and Rendahl, 1989).

Such an approach might obviously impact on the selection of researchers and the company's response to suggested inquiries. It might also help explain why I never received an answer to my request for interviewing SAS management about their perception of the strikes. Research reports do not always include reflections on why an organisation has chosen to participate, even if it might have considerably influenced results.

Planning the inquiry into the work of shop and security stewards was very much a question of negotiation. In the original project description from the union, they wanted to find out what a good educational programme is and how others (management, colleagues, and external partners) perceived the shop stewards and their role. Some of these questions are not feasible research questions (cf. Maxwell, 1996). It is not possible to find out what a good educational programme is, it is only possible to demonstrate that there might be different conceptions of what it would be. Respondents are not always able to say what additional education they need. Sometimes people lack the knowledge to describe what they are lacking.

Therefore, the inquiry ended up focusing on how the shop stewards experienced ongoing processes of change and any possible problems they might encounter in that connection. If educational planners know what the target group itself experiences as difficult in relation to concrete changes, they have a good indication of how to design a programme. How others perceived the shop stewards was given less priority. This might be important, but not as important as the eventual focus for the inquiry. However, this focus was only established following a prolonged discussion.

Good classic accounts on the question of access exist, and some have been referred to in the above. These have contributed significantly to the methodological literature by demonstrating the social contingencies surrounding qualitative studies. However, these accounts often present the problem of access as involving a negotiation between research interests, on the one hand, and organisational interests, on the other. Following contemporary Mode II knowledge production, however, the configuration of interests surrounding a qualitative inquiry will often be less bipolar and more complex.

Configurations of interest in relation to an inquiry

Evaluations can be examples of qualitative inquiries where it might not make sense to think in terms of bipolar interests. A particular department within an organisation might have as its specific task to evaluate other operational departments. Each of these have interests in relation to the evaluation, but these interests are broken down into the wish to obtain data to be used for internal learning processes and for external documentation, however, not documenting issues considered best left in the dark. And so on and so forth. Many different and cross-cutting interests are at stake, and these interests cannot be reduced to a simple confrontation between researcher and respondents.

Access, relations, and selection

The question of access to a field of study is not necessarily cleared just because initial formal negotiations have been completed. It continues to be an issue to a greater or lesser extent throughout the entire research process (Hammersley and Atkinson, 1987: 68), as different people and authorities decide on both their official and unofficial opinion about the inquiry. They classify the researcher in a particular way and relate to him or her on this basis.

It might be necessary to have double or triple rounds of negotiating the question of access (Hammersley and Atkinson, 1987), although it will often turn out that when opening up one gate, another is closing. (The fact that I had already obtained access to the organising committee might contribute to the fact that SAS management did not find it worthwhile to talk to me).

The access that has already been given can regulate what one is allowed to see in the field. Gatekeepers might consciously or subconsciously survey and control, as well as hinder or further, possible tracts for developing the inquiry. Gatekeepers might be happy to show you around, but they do it in a selective way (Turner, 1971: 124).

In the case from Borduria, the local partners in the project (who supplied me with an interpreter, driver, and logistic help) might in ways that were obscure to me have screened which places it was 'sensible' and 'possible' to visit. This affects the selection of case descriptions which form the basis for the display. I only control one part of the selection process, because I ask that we visit different types of farms, small and large, located at different places in the country, etc. At one time I ask to visit a particular farm which has been referred to by one of the respondents, but for obscure reasons my local contact person never really manages to contact this new place.

In the study of the shop stewards, the union took part in pointing out which companies and persons it might be interesting to study based on an idea of where 'things were happening'. Selection criteria were purposely biased towards companies undergoing major changes. I accepted these criteria because the theme for the entire inquiry was processes of change. Whether the selection was also biased in other ways, I do not know. But not all respondents were positive towards the union and its educational programme for shop and security stewards. So at least in this regard, no efficient conscious or subconscious censoring had taken place. I was actually happy with the selection because it showed great variation, and because the union showed a real openness and interest both with regard to convenient and less convenient results.

Some groups within a research field are harder than others to access 'in practice'. 'Practical limitations' are in fact often an indication of social structures. In other words, the history of access for the researcher in itself tells about social and cultural structures within the field of study. The fact that it is impossible to talk to farm workers without first asking the farm owner says a lot about the social situation for the farm workers (Hammersley and Atkinson, 1987: 69).

Meyerson (1991) researches different wards in a hospital. In some wards, each employee decides for him or herself whether they want to participate, in other wards everybody are ordered to partake. Meyerson includes this fact in his interpretation of data.

As a researcher, you will never know where the limits are to whom and what you may get access to unless you test these limits. However, testing these limits can also weaken relationships with key persons or gatekeepers, whose help you heavily depend on (Hammersley and Atkinson, 1987: 68).

A difficult group to access

During a study in Syldavia,[8] one of my assignments was to study the difficult relationship between four different groups of people within the villages: people of German origin, people of Hungarian origin, people of Rumanian origin, as well as 'Roma', which is the chosen name for the people we often call gypsies. 'Incidentally', 'practical' contingencies made it relatively easy to get into contact with the first three groups. They live centrally in the villages. Several hold official political office, and in some cases they have a kind of community centre with heating, where it is nice to sit as a visitor during winter. After a few days, my interpreter and I 'discovered' that the number of Roma respondents was dangerously close to zero after several days in the field. We decided to do something about it, and we explicitly asked our hosts (who were of German origin) about names or references for Roma we could speak to. We sensed that this request seemed a little ridiculous or embarrassing or irrelevant in their eyes, but – among others – we managed to get a description of the basket weaver, a Roma, who lived on the outskirts of the village. We could also take a walk in the part of the village where the Roma lived, it is easily recognisable, but it is easier to start a conversation if you have a name and a reference to go for.

Therefore, as part of the day's programme, we wanted to go and visit the basket weaver. We were told that we would be unlikely to find him at home, because he often walked about in the woods during the day searching for osiers for his baskets. So we spent the day doing other things. As it started getting dark, we again wanted to go and see him. We were told it was impractical to go out there in the dark. We insisted. A school teacher promised to take us, to make sure we would not get lost. As we came to the second last house before the basket weaver's there was still a way to go, and the school teacher pointed over a field, but discouraged us from going because of the mud, darkness, and bad weather. We lurched about a little, but finally ended up following his advice.

Instead, the school teacher asked a boy he met, and whom he knew from the school, to run out to the basket weaver and announce that we would like to talk to him. The basket weaver was to show up at the community centre (which belonged to the German-speaking community). We went back and had dinner. Later, there was a knock on the door. It was the basket weaver. I went out to talk to him. He had brought a new basket. We were sitting in a cold ante room. We had to, because the German-speaking community would not let him see what was inside the centre. The argument they gave was that he might return with

---

8   The fictional neighbouring country of Borduria.

Displaying Data 69

other Romas to steal whatever he saw. While we were sitting in the ante room speaking, the school teacher came out to us three times to tell me not to sit out there in the cold, but come inside to continue our cosy dinner. I politely declined each time, continuing my dialogue with the basket weaver, as long as I could think of good questions. Finally, the school teacher returned one more time, and the conversation was broken off. I thanked the basket weaver very much for his time and trouble. Humbly, the Roma gave the basket to the school teacher. Too late, I realised the truth, which the interpreter quickly explained. The basket weaver had brought the basket because he had believed the message was for him to come to the community centre because somebody wanted to buy a basket. As I had not struck a deal with him, in his humbleness, he had simply given the basket to the school teacher. Hurriedly, I asked my interpreter to run after the basket weaver so that he could at least explain him the truth and pay him for the basket. I went in to continue dinner with my hosts, where the mood had risen with good food, wine, and Gemütlichkeit.

The episode goes to show that cultural and structural relations within the village determine the practical conditions for my access to meet with the Roma.

These were simply examples. Obviously, a number of other conditions in relation to an inquiry are determining factors in deciding what data is generated, and consequently which displays might be the end result. For example:

- The overall purpose of the inquiry (Maxwell, 1996).

- The formulated research questions for the inquiry (Maxwell, 1996), both the explicit and implicit ones.

- The theoretical and conceptual orientation of the inquiry. Today, science, including qualitative inquiries, help shape, via the Pirandello-effect,[9] political and organisational reality. Therefore, scientific concepts often end up being political concepts (Latour, 1996; Beck, 1994).

- The researcher's preconception of the field of study. For example, the researcher might have chosen one or more organisations for closer examination based on a particular set of theoretical selection criteria (see for example Yin, 1984; or Lijphardt, 1971). At closer examination, it might turn out

---

9 Named after an Italian playwright renowned for plays where the audience continually influences the action by shouting to the actors.

that the chosen case more or less successfully fits the role it was supposed to have.

- The framework conditions for the inquiry, including money, time, financial sources, etc.

- The methodological design of the inquiry. What are the strengths and weaknesses of the chosen approach? Are weaknesses in the interview method compensated for by supplementing with observations, etc?

- The established framework for collecting data material, for example observation sheets, questionnaires, or interview guidelines etc.

- Note-taking during the inquiry process, for example divided into methodological, theoretical, and personal notes, as well as observational notes (Schatzmann and Strauss, 1973).

- The role of the researcher in the field (Hammersley and Atkinson, 1987; Wax, 1971).

- Interview data can be transcribed in different ways (Kvale, 1996).

- Data content can be condensed in different ways (Kvale, 1996). For example, the way that various interview statements have been condensed to a single key word to fit each cell in the matrix is a decisive factor in the SAS display.

- The mode of presentation sets its own terms of how to report the findings (Richardson, 2000).

The list of factors influencing the results of an inquiry can be continued indefinitely. There will always be factors influencing the factors that influence an inquiry.

In good qualitative inquiries, the researcher keeps as many of these factors in mind as possible, and notes down as many relevant ones as possible in a running research diary. We know that 'cognition follows the trail of action' (Weick, 1979), and therefore the researcher has to keep track of those trails of action his or her understanding develops along during the inquiry.

Displaying Data 71

No diary is an ultimate proof of the truth.

On his journey to what was later to become known as America, Columbus kept two different diaries. One he showed his crew, in which he noted down fewer nautical miles than they had in fact travelled. The other diary was kept secret from the crew. In this, he noted down the correct distances and other things he did not wish to share with the crew. One of the major reasons for this double entry book-keeping was that several members of the crew were uneasy about travelling too far from home, and also worried that they might fall over the edge when reaching the end of the world. The secret diary may have served as a basis for Columbus' briefing of Queen Isabella and King Ferdinand, but it has been lost to posterity. However, a paraphrase of a copy exists, and on this basis a reconstruction has been made (Kjærsgaard, 1991).

The example shows that different diaries can be written with a different audience in mind. No diary is an ultimate proof of the truth.

In the diary, the researcher accounts for the history of his or her inquiry. However, this is a paradoxical demand to make, if it is made entirely without qualifications. No system is able to report everything about itself (Bateson, 1972). When a researcher has to account for his/her 'cognition', he or she will do so based on the point currently reached on his/her 'trail of action'. Insights and wild goose chases are defined by the interpretation they will subsequently be given from a point down the trail. Cognitive developments obviously form the basis for the subsequent writing process, but the flow of the final text will rarely follow the cognitive process in its precise logical and chronological development (Hammersley and Atkinson, 1987: 204). The cognitive process has itself been developed further before you reach the writing phase, and the writing process in itself both adds and subtracts issues. The reporting is never entirely complete.

Nevertheless, the ideal of a relatively self-explanatory display holds sway, even if it may never be completely regarded in isolation from the context of the inquiry. The display helps both the researcher and the reader of an inquiry focus their thoughts on the relevant issues. It points out a 'text' where the conditions and contingencies of the inquiry can be regarded as 'context'. It is both possible and fruitful to focus on *what* the display shows, even if the answer to *why* it shows this has to be sought in the framework conditions for making the display.

As I prefer to put it (it will be explained in greater detail in the final chapter), the researcher has to report his findings in a rigorous manner, but this rigour floats around in a sea of contingent factors characteristic of a particular research process. All this, however, does not subtract value from the important point that even in the face of these contingencies, it is still possible to focus on an (albeit local) rigour in presenting the data. A display can be an excellent tool to maintain such rigour.

CHAPTER 4
Quality Criteria in Qualitative Inquiries

> *...the most crucial of these simple virtues, namely honesty: 'I will not deceive and, above all, I will not deceive myself', in its negativity, its moderation and temperance, this exemplary rule more or less covers all other rules within the base ethic of scientific work.*
>
> Lars-Henrik Schmidt[1]

> *The truth cannot float. It lies on the ground in front of our feet, donkeys and people trample upon it and soil it, but this is of no consequence; it remains on the ground, in one sense it is the ground itself, suspended underneath us like a safety net, we will never be able to fall beneath it. Therefore, we have nothing to fear. It is not possible to fail.*
>
> Thorkild Hansen in "Arabia Felix: The Danish Expedition of 1761-1767"

The characteristics of qualitative inquiries – a flow sheet

The rules for displaying qualitative data I suggested in the previous chapter, should preferably confer with a set of criteria for good qualitative research. Therefore, I will use this chapter to present and discuss such criteria.

My ambition is limited. I do not intent to once and for all present the ultimate set of quality criteria for research work, subsequent to which all discussions of the subject will end. Such a set of criteria would presuppose that we were able to transcend our limitations as creators of knowledge bounded by time and space (Schwandt, 2002: 105).

---
1 Schmidt, 2000: 247.

Instead, it is possible to compare such criteria with criteria for moral conduct in different life situations. Many life situations are so complex and filled with dilemmas that it is not morally possible to find a 'solution' based on a particular criterion; each situation has to be decided upon in a practical way. In other words, the individual situation can be richer and more complex than was presupposed, if one carries ambitions for a universal set of criteria. Likewise, a given scientific methodological problem will never be fully described simply by referring to a set of criteria for good methodology. In brief, it is impossible to avoid a discussion of the relationship between criteria and the complexity of the concrete situation. Criteria are interesting and worth paying attention to. But they do not provide closure to the discussion about what good science (good methodology, good morals, etc.) is.

Thus, my ambition is simply to suggest a set of preliminary criteria which seem reasonable, and which may have a certain beneficial effect on a series of local situations – and to show that my suggestion about making displays is consistent with such a set of reasonable criteria.

In my deduction of quality criteria for qualitative research, I aim to take my starting point, as far as possible, in the essential characteristics of this type of work.

In the introduction, qualitative method was delimited on the basis that it is a type of inquiry one chooses when the most important categories of the inquiry have not been predetermined, but on the contrary are developed as a consequence of the inquiry itself. The researcher wants to find out how people from category A relate to phenomenon B, but does not yet know anything about the nature of this relationship.

Consequently, a flexible design is used. The design – including the identification of the main categories of the inquiry and the concrete way of asking questions – is further developed throughout the inquiry.

Quality Criteria in Qualitative Inquiries 75

Figure 4.1. A flow sheet showing the development of a qualitative inquiry.

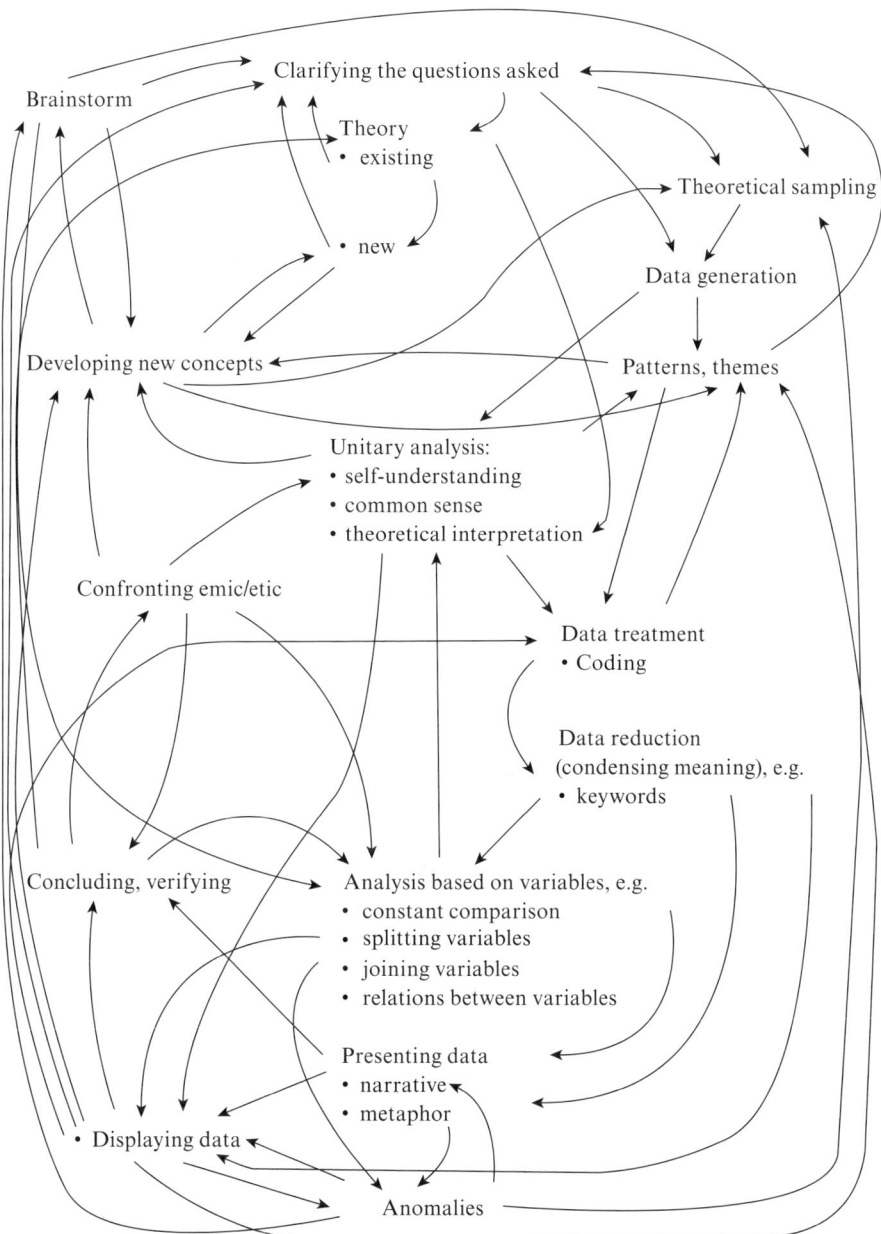

At first sight, the many arrows make up a confusing image. Of course, not all inquiries will follow all arrows. The flow sheet is not an algorithm which prescribes how to carry out automatically the research process. The course of each individual arrow is not crucial. The flow sheet is in invitation to consider the nature of the research process, including the fact that the process contains several loops. Towards the end of this section, I will express this fact more precisely in theoretical terms, and derive implications for how to assess quality in qualitative method. But first I wish to develop a step by step image of the qualitative research process, both touching upon simple and complex processes, describing the various steps along the way.

In the simplest form of research process, the researcher starts by clarifying the questions that are asked, then generates data and carries out a unitary analysis, for example by learning about a phenomenon in the life world of one respondent at a time. Statements by the respondent are analysed by putting them in relation to that person's self-understanding, a common sense interpretation, and a theoretical interpretation (Kvale 1996: chapter 12). Data is treated and coded (Glaser and Strauss, 1967), and subsequently reduced by condensing meaning in keywords. Data is presented for example in the form of a narrative/ story, a summarising metaphor, or a graphic display. The researcher concludes and verifies, and then refers back to theory on the basis of the analysis – and he/she has an answer for the questions asked. In this simplified version, a qualitative inquiry resembles an almost perfect circle; like the movement of the little hand on a dial in the course of an hour. (And it resembles a textbook plan for a corresponding quantitative inquiry).

But qualitative inquiries rarely behave like this in practice. The story of the simple, forward moving process on the dial is inconsistent with the actual practice of qualitative inquiries, because it ignores exactly those moments when the qualitative inquiry becomes instructive and reflexive, and when the design is further developed. For example, patterns and themes are discovered during data generations which are interpreted theoretically, leading to new questions already during the actual interview. When treating data, it is necessary continually to return to the unitary analysis. When presenting data, it is common to come across negative or deviating results, requiring a new selection of additional data to cover the holes and explain anomalies (Maaløe, 1996: 236).

Likewise, concluding and verifying are not isolated steps in the process; they interplay with several other steps. For example, it is possible to confront *etic* and *emic* perspectives (etic is the perspective of the outside interpreter, emic is the respondent's categories (Vidich and Lyman, 2000)) – or, as Berger and Kellner (1982) put it, the sociological second order interpretation has to be respectful of the respondent's own everyday typifications. If discordances occur, it may lead to a renewed look upon interpretations of data.

An analysis based on variables may come into the picture, for example as a result of a particular reduction of data or efforts towards verification. In a variable-based analysis, phenomena are compared across research units. It is possible to carry out *constant comparisons* (Glaser and Strauss, 1967) of traits and sub-traits of various situations or persons, you can split a variable[2] into a series of specified sub-variables, you can join a number of variables into one superior factor, or you can determine the relations between variables more specifically (Miles and Huberman, 1994: 187). This, too, can lead to new ways of reducing and coding data, new patterns and themes, etc.

In other words, the qualitative inquiry continually revisits itself. It develops as a function of its own observations. It may encounter a crisis. It may lead to new insights that run so much counter to previous assumptions that it becomes extremely difficult not to sense one has reached a deadlock. Nevertheless, the inquiry process is often capable of overcoming its crises; when moving from one step in the process to another, the picture is stirred, because previous insights are put into a more or less new framework. When viewed in this light, crises are actually not so bad. It is the crises that make the research process relate to itself once again.

A little exercise based on figure 4.1

1. Where do many of the arrows start?

2. Where do many of the arrows end?

3. Is it possible to go directly from data generation to an analysis based on variables?

Even if the flow sheet could have been drawn in several other ways, the answers to these questions are actually quite telling. 'Many arrows starting' may be understood as a 'good starting point for further work', and 'many arrows ending' may be understood as a 'solution to several problems'.

---

2   The term variable is used here broadly to denote phenomena which are characterized by variation.

Draw your own research process

Here is a second display of the analytic process, this time without the arrows. Insert your own, to make a drawing of your analytic process.

	Clarifying the questions asked	
Brainstorm		
	Theory	
	• existing,	
		Theoretical sampling
	• new	
Developing new concepts		Data generation
		Patterns, themes
	Unitary analysis:	
	• self-understanding	
	• common sense	
	• theoretical interpretation	
Confronting emic/etic		
		Data treatment
		• Coding
		Data reduction
		(condensing meaning),
		• e.g. keywords
Concluding, verifying	Analysis based on variables e.g.	
	• constant comparison	
	• splitting variables	
	• joining variables	
	• relations between variables	
	Presenting data	
	• narrative	
	• metaphor	
Displaying data		
	Anomalies	

Theoretically, it is possible to describe the qualitative research process as an autopoietic system. Autopoietic systems are defined by their own ability to generate those elements they need to maintain their organisation (Kneer and Nassehi, 1993: 55). They function recursively, i.e. they continually use products and results of their own operations as the basis for their further operation. Autopoietic systems do come into contact with the outside world, but their openness towards the environment is determined by the way the system closes in on itself through its self-reference. The fact that the autopoietic system is closed in a particular way, is exactly the precondition for its way of opening itself up in a particular way. It is open towards outside 'irritations', but these irritations are defined by the system via their place in the continual autopoiesis of the system.

This observation harbours a far-reaching epistemological consequence: perception is no longer an adequate reflection of the outside world, but rather the *internal* systemic construction of an *external* world.

The question is, whether it is possible to determine any quality criteria for qualitative research work on this basis.

Quality criteria in qualitative inquiries

If data in a qualitative inquiry cannot be regarded as reflections of the outside world, but only as systemic constructions that are internal to the inquiry process, it becomes impossible to uphold the correspondence criterion.

The correspondence criterion

This is a simple and classic criterion, according to which the truth value of a statement simply depends on the statement's correspondence with reality. But even if this criterion at first sight seems innocent enough, it quickly runs into trouble (Williams and May, 1996: 37). The most important problem is that we do not have direct unmediated access to reality, but can only access it via other inquiries that produce other statements. These statements, too, are system internal constructions, occurring in other inquiry systems. In other words, it may be necessary – or at least of great practical advantage – to abstain from appealing to reality when assessing qualitative inquiries.

The replication criterion

Thus, it would be impossible to imagine a test situation where one compares a statement from a qualitative inquiry with reality itself. One may compare a statement with other statements on the same issue. In reality, however, this is not as straightforward as it may sound. First of all, the various statements actually compared have to relate to the same issue. One may for example question whether two different inquiries within the same organisation, one based on a structural perspective and the other on a cultural perspective, actually deal with the same issues. The answer to this question remains unclear if one practices 'passive perspectivism' (Schmidt, quoted in Pedersen and Larsen, 1995) – that is, describes the object of the inquiry alternately from one angle and another, without paying attention to how each perspective is co-constitutive for the actual object of inquiry. Hence, to test one statement against another is only possible if they are not actually statements about different matters.

But in the absence of major sources of incorrectness in those other statements we use to control our original statement, we may, after all, find a certain degree of affirmation in the fact that another inquiry system can replicate a given inquiry and reach the same results. It is possible to talk about a replication criterion. Data is reliable if it can be reproduced when another inquiry repeats the procedure of an existing inquiry.

In practice, however, the replication criterion is often somewhat unworldly, because an entirely identical inquiry of the exact same object is impossible in reality. Furthermore, within qualitative inquiries, the replication criterion is often unrealistic even in theory, because the qualitative inquiry is based on the understanding that reality is highly likely to change as a result of being inquired into. There is often a rather close relationship between the object of inquiry and the researcher him or herself. For example in cases of sustained fieldwork. This will necessarily affect the research field. The qualitative interview may be regarded as an interpersonal relation, often leading to new insights and emotional reactions (Kvale, 1996: 34). The significance of the themes changes for the interviewee as a result of the interview, and the interviewee changes as a person.[3] Consequently, it would be unfair to demand that a subsequent inquiry into the same themes and the same person would yield the same results.

The reliability criterion

This means that data in principle are reliable if and when they are produced using instruments that are reliable. Reliability can be tested through whether another inquiry in principle would be able to reproduce the same data, without necessarily imagining that such a second inquiry will ever actually be carried out. The reliability criterion is familiar to us from common teaching in quantitative methodology. The criterion is slightly more difficult to impose in qualitative inquiries, because these are so deeply immersed in those social contexts in which they take place. In terms of collecting data, a survey-based inquiry can be carried out by posting a standardised questionnaire in the mail; whereas a qualitative inquiry is based on several hours of strongly personalised

---

3   This is for example true for extensive fieldwork.

and highly contextual interaction between researcher and field. The number of relationships that need to be described to give a sufficiently full account of a data collection situation, so that for example a certain way of asking questions is reliable – i.e. that it would produce the same answers, and thereby data, in another similar situation – is simply foreboding. In this connection, it would also be necessary to include the prior theoretical understanding of the researcher. Altogether, this makes the reliability criterion rather abstract in connection with qualitative inquiries. On second thought, it is also formalistic and lacking content. It does not suffice that a certain instrument for data collection in principle can produce the same data in a different inquiry. Preferably, it should also be data that are correct in their content, are telling, interesting, etc. In other words, data have to live up to a validity criterion. This may take on several shapes, for example in the form of communicative validity.

Communicative validity

Communicative validity concerns the question of whether a statement from an inquiry can stand the test of a subsequent dialogue. It is possible to think of different participants in such a dialogue.

1. First of all, it is possible to carry out a 'member check', a 'confrontation with emic categories', or a 'respondent validation' (Hammersley and Atkinson, 1987: 187) in relation to the 'interpretive schemes' of the objects of the inquiry themselves (Jones, 1983: 151). In other words, comparing statements from the inquiry with viewpoints and perspectives among those persons participating in the inquiry. The ideal is that the researcher's interpretation should be *sinnadequat*, i.e. adequate in terms of the meanings characteristic of the lifeworld of the respondent (Berger and Kellner, 1982: 45). However, interviewees do not always wish to stand by their statements. Maybe they cannot or will not recognise their statements in the form they take on in the inquiry.

> ### *A problem concerning respondent validation*
>
> Upon receiving a word-by-word transcript of his own interview statements, a high-ranking public official strongly objected to them. This was most likely due to the fact that written documents within his organisational culture could have serious consequences which he did not imagine when expressing himself orally.

Obviously, this type of validation only applies to one part of the inquiry, namely the part that focuses on understanding and summarising the first order constructions (emic categories) of the stakeholders themselves. The question of whether the inquiry adequately transforms and integrates these constructions within a theoretical second order interpretation, is not something you can reasonably expect the stakeholders themselves to relate to, let alone accept.

It is common for qualitative analyses, for example cultural analyses, to be based on a premiss of explicating that which is implicit for the stakeholders; to reveal the constructed nature of an apparently solid reality (Berger and Luckmann, 1979), to theoretically recognise that which is culturally misrecognised (Bourdieu 1977), and to theoretically misrecognise that which is otherwise commonly recognised. When viewed in this perspective, it is utterly unreasonable to presuppose, expect, or aim for solidarity between the results of the inquiry and the life perspective of the participants themselves. But the question of whether the inquiry operates with a correct understanding of emic categories as a precondition for the theoretical analysis may, of course, be validated via a dialogue with the participants. This point actually becomes clearer by dispensing with the concepts of emic and etic, which are familiar to us from anthropology and ethnography, and instead use Schutz and Berger's (Berger and Kellner, 1982) concepts of first order and second order typifications. The theoretical interpretations – the second order constructions – are not simply 'different' from the stakeholders' own first order constructions. On the contrary, the theoretical concepts are concentrations and abstractions which contain the every-day constructions within them, only at another level, a 'second order' level.

2. Secondly, statements may be tested through a discussion with a community of researchers sharing the theoretical and methodological assumptions of the inquiry. Would a researcher, working on the same research question and with knowledge of the theoretical starting point, be able to acknowledge the validity of statements from this inquiry? The question is not whether the same inquiry can or should be repeated, but rather whether its results follow from their theoretical and methodological foundations, which in turn are meaningful and possible to support on the basis of a scientific criterion of relevance (Berger and Kellner, 1982). This does not provide a guarantee, but nevertheless, it is always possible to argue for and against a given interpretation on a sensible basis.

We can, however, qualify the criterion of communicative validity if we recall the fact that the inquiry's image of reality is not in direct correspondence with reality, but rather a representation produced internally in a system. Consequently, the inputs coming from interviewees and scientific colleagues are not really external inputs, but irritations that the system only allows itself to be open towards qua its closure. An inquiry process thus 'lets in' various statements from stakeholders in selected ways at selected points in time. The same observation holds good for theoretical statements from books, colleagues, etc. A research process thereby reproduces its own version of the scientific nature it claims to posses. This does not, however, imply that any version of scientific character carries equally great chances of being recognised. An inquiry itself is part of a greater system, a scientific system, which simultaneously carries out its own contextual openings and closures in relation to individual inquiries. Not all inquiries acquire the same scientific standing and recognition.

But back on track: we still lack a criterion, one which does not depend on an 'external' reality to legitimate the inquiry on the basis of a correspondence with this reality, one which describes the representations of the 'external' as also always already 'internal representations'. This criterion has to be able to describe how the research process relates to those 'openings' which it is aware are actually constructed by itself. It is a criterion which is concerned with the quality of the process whereby these internal representations are created.

Validity through good craftsmanship

It is possible to assess an inquiry on the basis of *the validity of its craftsmanship*. This criterion has to do with the skill in handling the method in relation to the material. First of all, the criterion is about establishing whether the methods have been applied in a reasonable manner – in detail – in relation to the concrete field of study; whether a tool is used according to its purpose; whether one finishes the job even if results turn out to be inconvenient; whether one systematically attempts to eliminate any source of invalidity that might turn up; whether the validity of the work is tested by oneself. This is done by continually testing, asking questions, and conceptualising (Kvale, 1996: 242-44). This criterion is about how a research system itself relates to those internal representations it creates. It is possible to understand the idea of validity through good craftsmanship as a kind of communicative validity, in the sense that it is the auto-communication of the research process which is in focus.

In other words, we are getting nearer our goal of finding a quality criterion which concerns the research process, rather than whether the research results correspond with a given external reality. At the same time, we are closing in on a criterion which may assess the scientific nature of the research process. To be scientific is not a question of the reality of the inquiry, nor its field of study (which may be anything), but a question of how the research process is carried out.

On this basis, quality is not only an attribute of the results. Quality does not inhere in an individual point or an individual phase in the research work, but in the way the entire process is carried out. Good craftsmanship therefore becomes a joint concept for the quality of the inquiry; within it we may find other more partial types of validity, for example respondent validation.

Good craftsmanship is a superior *procedural quality* pertaining to the integrity of the research process. And the quality of the research is *contextual*, i.e. it does not depend on a prior check list, but is the result of a meeting between methodological competency and concrete challenges from the field.

The validity stemming from good craftsmanship is most easily obtained if one applies methods that are based on knowledge acquired through scientific schooling (from courses, books, previous inquiries, the entire scientific methodological tradition). But we cannot expect the application of a concrete methodological process to live up to a predefined check list. It has to be attuned to the field of study, including the way the field appears as already having been studied at a given point of time during the inquiry. Consequently, the criterion of good craftsmanship does not lead to a rapid closure of the discussion of validity, it is rather simply a way of discussing the issue.

Neither extreme relativism nor fixed check lists help us here. Reasonable arguments do.

The transparency criterion

The *transparency* criterion is a classic methodological criterion, which in the light of the criterion of good craftsmanship acquires new significance. The transparency criterion implies that the methodological approach has to be explicitly put forward, simply to ensure that it is possible to see what has been going on during an inquiry.

This means that the transparency criterion works as a precondition for several other criteria, for example the replication criterion, the reliability criterion, and the criterion of communicative validity. It only makes sense to consider repeating an inquiry, assessing its reliability, and discussing it thoroughly among colleagues, if the approach that was taken has been explicitly described. But the transparency criterion also stands in a fruitful relationship with the notion of validity through good craftsmanship. Good craftsmanship in itself promotes transparency. Reversely, transparency exposes methodological problems and anomalies, which provide energy to a validation based on good craftsmanship. In other words, the transparency criterion does not only have a role to play *externally* when assessing an inquiry, transparency may also provide new life to the internal development of the inquiry. This does not mean that a research system will ever become completely transparent to itself – this is simply not possible according to Bateson (1972) and Kneer and Nassehi (1993). Some of the best challenges you can pose to a research process which attempt to reach scientific status is: 'try to be explicit', and 'work on being transparent to yourself'.

Finally a few comments on two criteria that are sometimes mentioned in discussions of qualitative method.

The heuristic criterion

The *heuristic* criterion concerns the question of whether the inquiry has succeeded in obtaining new knowledge, insights, and perspectives. Several social scientific studies, both classical ones and those contemporary ones which create debate, are characterised by scoring high on a heuristic criterion – a sociological vision, a far reaching conceptual development, a surprising way of putting things into perspective. The imaginative and creative side of science has tended to be overlooked within certain traditions – not least among those carrying on a positivistic heritage, which is based on a sharp division between, on the one hand, rigorous empirical work and a 'context of justification' which lives up to scientific rules, and, on the other hand, the 'context of discovery'; a distant wonderland from which good hypotheses appear on the basis of the aimless fantasising of the researcher, a wonderland which obviously is beyond any kind of scientific description.

Such a sharp division, however, is difficult to uphold in practice. The good idea leading to new insights – the imagination – is a far more important component in science than we are often led to believe (Morin, 1990; Nisbet, 1976).

It has often been emphasised within the history of qualitative method that we need to think of 'context of discovery and context of justification' as standing in a closer relationship to one another. How the researcher acts and how the researcher thinks in a qualitative inquiry become closely interconnected in the light of the 'worldliness' of science – its close relation to concrete social practice. Glaser and Strauss' (1967) idea of 'grounded theory' is an influential exponent of this notion: Scientific concepts and ideas occur on the basis of a constantly searching and reflexive empirical practice. Hypotheses need to be 'grounded'. Even if Glaser and Strauss' notion of ideas more or less jumping from data and into the open consciousness of the researcher seems outdated, the close connection between good ideas and empirical practice remains a core idea within qualitative method. There is a dynamic interplay between fostering good ideas and working on data. This means that the heuristic criterion and validity acquired through good craftsmanship are intimately dependent on one another – even if they analytically may be regarded as two different concepts.

Pragmatic validity

Pragmatic validity concerns what value you place on an inquiry, depending on its practical utility. The inquiry is assessed on the basis of whether it leads to change in actions carried out, in social practices, or in the life situation of stakeholders. But surely the actual inquiry itself represents an action? Unless one operates with a curious distinction between 'real actions' on the one hand, and 'non-real ones' on the other. What is worse, the criterion of pragmatic validity is a downright alien criterion in relation to scientific validity criteria. An inquiry may lead to more or fewer actions than anticipated, without this being attributable to the inquiry itself. When politicians for example claim that an inquiry is 'useless', it is more often a question of political unwillingness to change, rather than a question of the actual quality of the inquiry.

The most basic problem in relation to pragmatic validity is how to assess any action an inquiry may lead to. This presupposes normative assessments which do not follow logically from scientific work, and which may often actually corrupt an inquiry process if they are turned into a goal for the processes as a whole. A pragmatic criterion for the little boy's inquiry into the emperor's new clothes would have ensured that the emperor could have completed his procession without being made a laughing stock.

Good inquiries often have a critical edge. But they only genuinely acquire this edge when methodological skill and integrity in themselves ensure that established images and understandings are challenged, and not simply because the inquiry in advance is designed to be 'critical'. If one knows in advance that an inquiry will be critical, and one knows what critical means, who is supposed to be critical of the so-called critics?

Display of the described criteria

Recommended criteria
Validity through good craftsmanship, which is often promoted by or promotes
- Communicative validity
- Transparency
- The heuristic criterion

Criteria which are not particularly recommended
- Correspondence
- Replication
- Reliability
- Pragmatic validity

In this way, we end up with a preference for a validity criterion based on good craftsmanship. And we note that communicative validity plays a certain role, not least in connection with good craftsmanship; and the heuristic criterion often follows suit. We also recommend the transparency criterion, not least because it supports the two others.

This position is entirely consistent with the skill, communication, and transparency involved in making displays as suggested in the previous chapter.

CHAPTER 5
Contingency and Rigour in Knowledge Production

> *Devotees of science a long time ago gave up the idea of a final, untouchable truth, the precise image of 'reality', which was waiting to be revealed just around the next corner.*
> Francois Jacob[1]

> *It is exactly our actual engagement with the world which orients all our conceptual fixations.*
> Maurice Merleau-Ponty[2]

The strategy for this chapter is to account for two apparently opposing conditions for scientific knowledge production: contingency and rigour. I wish to cultivate each separately, and subsequently show how they are connected. The format focuses on specific points connected along a few conceptual lines. I will sometimes make use of secondary sources. This final chapter is not to be regarded as an independent scientific philosophical account. The joint function of the chapter is to demonstrate that the view taken on rules for displaying data and on quality criteria in qualitative method, as presented in chapters 3 and 4, is consistent with considerations in philosophy of science.

Contingency

The notion of progress has been prevalent for centuries in the history of the West (Nisbet, 1980), and a central ingredient in this notion has been the idea of objective and secure scientific knowledge production.

The modern scientific understanding of certain knowledge production is

---

1 Jacob, 1985: 13. Author's translation.
2 Merleau-ponty, 1969: 33.

not least precipitated by Descartes, who introduces his own subjective doubt as an absolutely secure foundation for science. Simultaneously, Descartes presents a concept of the subject as possessor of knowledge in its 'pure subject' form, which is abstracted and isolated from the world. The ideal consists in a clear division between subject and object, the knower from the known. At the same time, the ideal is an expression of the hope to procure a secure source of knowledge. Even if he precipitated the change, Descartes was unlikely to know that this new type of knowledge, scientific knowledge, was about to attempt to overthrow the authority of religion as the secure foundation for knowledge.

Subsequently, philosophy of science has made its own contribution to overthrowing the notion of secure foundations, and particularly within the last century or so, philosophy of science has engaged in a prolonged and continually more thorough depletion of 'reality', a prolonged and far-reaching tale of more and more worrying problems concerning the notion of objective and secure knowledge.

In brief, we have come to the realisation that knowledge production does not happen on the basis of a secure and incontrovertible foundation, but rather is fundamentally dependent on its starting point, be it socially, historically, culturally, linguistically, epistemologically, or institutionally etc. determined. In brief, knowledge production is contingent. Contingent is not the same as random (even if it is sometimes interpreted this way), but circumstantial in the following sense: dependent on conditions, defined by situations; i.e. precisely not random, even if there may be several and complex ways of defining the situation, and it may not always be easy to see through these definitions. The word contingency also covers the meaning that defining situational conditions could have been different. That which is contingent is dependent on something else. It is neither random nor decided by fate.

The fact that knowledge production is contingent, is to a large extent received wisdom within qualitative method (even if this received wisdom sometimes leads to mistaken implications). But I wish to use this chapter to put contingency into play in relation to another substantiated basic condition for scientific knowledge production: rigour. Hopefully, this will lead to insights which are not to the same extent received wisdom within qualitative method. But let me begin by emphasising that I do not in any way aim to question contingency as a basic condition. It is a great gift for researchers to have discovered this. The question is how to interpret it, and whether it is understood together with the concept of rigour, and which implications the relation between the two has for the practice of qualitative method.

The active role of consciousness in knowledge production

Modern science has to a large extent aimed for consciousness to be able to understand the laws of nature as directly as possible. Kant, however, is among the first to point out that the understanding of such laws presupposes certain fundamental mental categories such as time, space, and causality (Tarnas, 1996: 343). Consciousness is already organised in a certain way which structures understanding. Man is only able to apprehend things the way they appear to human consciousness, not the things in themselves. The question remains how these pre-structured categories themselves are constituted.

Phenomenologists harbour the same thought – that it is impossible to say anything meaningful about the thing in itself, but only about how it appears to consciousness (Psathas, 1973). Consciousness is playing its own game. Phenomenologists realise that consciousness co-constructs the whole concept of a dog, even if you only observe half a dog viewed from the side. Visual impressions can vary greatly, and yet consciousness constructs a dog. The patterns of recognition within consciousness are both self-activating and pliable (Morin, 1990: 121), cp. the example from chapter 3 with the three lines at the Experimentarium in Copenhagen; three lines which consciousness itself puts together to form a triangle.

One of the great phenomenologists, Husserl, operates with a subject which others criticise for still resembling the Cartesian subject too much in its isolation from the outer world. Other phenomenologists (for example Merleau-Ponty), however, do not hesitate to ground the subject as embedded in the world. All that I know, I know by virtue of the viewpoint which is mine, Merleau-Ponty writes (1969) and that which orients all our conceptual fixations is exactly our actual engagement in the world (1969: 33). Consciousness is not simply a consciousness *of* the world, but also very importantly a consciousness *in* the world (Merleau-Ponty, 1978).

The subject is grounded in the world, not least bodily. 'The place my body takes up in this world is the starting point from which I orient myself in space' Schutz writes (1975: 34); and when the subject aims to understand something, it does so on the basis of its own labour. The body and the world are simultaneous aspects of the same phenomenon, a corporeality (Fontana and Frey, 1994: 125). The bodily foundations for knowledge production remind us of some of the ways in which we are excited and tired by knowledge production, and the way in which we may adhere to ideas in the same way that living bodies adhere to that which they care for (Morin, 1990: 109 and 148). There are limits to rationality, also within knowledge production. Consciousness plays its own games within understanding, and consciousness itself is bodily tied down to the world.

Statements expressed by consciousness are untrustworthy

Another contribution casting doubts on notions of security and objectivity in knowledge production has come from Marx, Freud, and Durkheim, who each have shown how consciousness is influenced by larger factors which it cannot control, much less apprehend. Marx has thus pointed out how consciousness is determined by work and class relations, and especially how these relations possibly may lead to a false consciousness, i.e. ideologically mistaken views.

Durkheim and Freud have together precipitated the breakthrough of symbolism in our understanding of man, through the notion that man only to a very limited degree is the master of his consciousness in terms of instrumentality, rationality, or transparency. Durkheim demonstrates that human consciousness is merely a small part of a larger societal collective consciousness. In addition, Freud shows how human consciousness is secretly controlled by strong, subconscious, symbolic powers. It becomes increasingly untenable to trust the human apprehension of the world as a reflection of things as they are (Tarnas, 1996: 353). 'Below, what we are pleased to regard as our most profound spiritual and moral insight, lies a seething cauldron of power motives, economic interests, and selfish fantasies' (Douglas, 1986: 81).

And it becomes increasingly difficult to hold on to a belief which used to characterise modernity, namely that the conscious reflection of man would enable him to master his life circumstances and his conditions once again. Both Marx, Freud, and Durkheim are specifically modern thinkers, and consequently they naturally each suggest possible ways out of the miseries they identify. If one is modern, one has to attempt to master the great powers invisibly influencing consciousness. But these three great modern classics also clearly identify the hardships of this process, a theme which is subsequently taken up by other thinkers. It will become obvious that it is increasingly difficult for man, and increasingly unclear how, to reconcile these great powers (in addition, very unpleasant powers) which psychologically, institutionally, culturally, and socially form human consciousness.

Language contributes to understanding

With a starting point in research into native American languages, it has been observed how vocabulary and basic grammatical structures differ greatly between languages. And to a large extent, language predetermines possibilities for apprehension. Based on this, two American scientists – who are inspired both by anthropology, linguistics, and philosophy – have reached the so-called Sapir-Whorf-thesis, namely that language conditions thinking. This provides various possibilities for understanding within each linguistic circle, but only possibilities put at man's disposable by the language in question. When Eskimos for example have 24 different words for snow, and Hopi Indians use one word for all flying animals, humans, and objects, this is a reflection of how differently language makes us understand, interpret, and organise our world. This leads to the observation that we may expect insurmountable problems of translation from one linguistic circle to another (Asad, 1986).

Language is much more than a tool. If language were only a tool and did not have a poetic dimension, it would be much more in line with reality than it actually is (Langer, 1957: 36). Language constructs a symbolic world. It is first and foremost a mythical construct, and secondly it is a tool (Langer, 1957; Cassirer, 1946).

De Saussure (1959) points out how the signification of words is determined by their differences rather than their relation to reality. When certain significations have been formed, the formation of other significations becomes logical and expectable. To put it abstractly in Castoriadis' words, the significations of language have a set-identical dimension, where categories are logically ordered, and certain things are predictable once one is familiar with other facts; but language as a totality rests above all on an imaginary dimension – it is able to name cultural constructs without a physical correlate (Castoriadis, 1987). The individual signification is dependent on other significations, but the significations as a totality make up an invention of the world which cannot be reduced to something else.

As soon as the signifying universe of the language is in place, it will enter the scene as an unavoidable symbolic universe standing between man and his surroundings (Cassirer, 1965). Like other objectified factors in society, language possesses a factuality, and externality, and an almost compulsory character, a 'choseité' in the words of Durkheim (Berger, 1970). It has not been chosen by the individual. As Durkheim pointed out – the same Durkheim who more than any other constituted the sociological perspective as a scientific one – he did not each morning decide to speak French. The French language was an existing reality prior to any sort of 'rational' choice of language contemplated by Durkheim.

Language preconditions our understanding. 'By the same process whereby he spins language out of his being, he also ensnares himself in it'; consequently, each language draws a magical circle around the people it belongs to (Cassirer, 1946: 9). 'Every society meets a new idea with its own concepts, its own tacit fundamental way of seeing things; that is to say, with its own questions, its peculiar curiosity' (Langer, 1957: 6).

Meaning and understanding

The category of *meaning* and its methodological counterpart *Verstehen* (understanding) are necessary keys to access such symbolic universes. The discovery of the category of meaning as fundamental to the study of the human – and its migration from peripheral to central category in connection with the entire 'interpretive turn' in large segments of the social and cultural sciences (Geertz, 1975: 29) – has had its own contingency-enhancing effects on scientific knowledge production. It has become even more difficult to trust the existence of absolute and secure knowledge.

The introduction of the category of meaning alleviates the problem that modern natural scientific cosmology has been found incapable of understanding man himself based on his primary qualities as a social, political, historical being (Luckmann, 1978), and as a thinking self (Morin, 1981). Instead, man has been reduced to an abstract and mechanic conglomerate of factors and biological mechanisms. This has led to two different 'solutions', either a violent reduction of the image of man as exactly an assemblage of mechanisms, or an exclusion of the specifically human from scientific studies (Luckmann, 1978).

Introducing categories like meaning and interpretation by Dilthey, Webers, and Schutz is a counteracting attempt to insist on a non-reductionist image of that which is specifically human, and simultaneously study man as an object of scientific inquiry and reflection. As an aside, it should be mentioned that this way of thinking often has led to a kind of negotiated cease fire between the natural sciences, applying the method of 'explaining', on the one hand, and the human sciences on the other, applying the method of 'understanding'. As if the biologists and medical students were given the body, while the cultural researchers could deal with epistemological and cognitive aspects; a division which seems unnecessarily artificial, both in the light of the research object and in the light of philosophy of science. But this way of attributing the category of meaning a space within the vocabulary of human sciences has at least saved man from the prospect of only being able to describe himself as a rather monstrous being (even if the purely mechanical models still are being glorified, lately for example by brain researchers claiming to be able to explain anything ranging from substance abuse to psychological deviations based on chemical variations and electric activity registered on scanning images).

The category of meaning indicates how the creation of meaning is a very central task for man, a task which cannot be reduced to needs fulfilment, survival, interests, chemicals, or other basic principles. On the contrary, any universe of meaning rests, besides the set-identical dimension (identifiable logics and differences), on a fundamental imaginary dimension (Castoriadis, 1987). This latter dimension implies the creation of a social and cultural world.

To understand a given universe of world innovation, it is necessary to do some interpretive work, which for example is expressed in Weber's (1946) conception of understanding as a method. But the job of interpreting is fundamentally based on the ability to show an accommodating interest in reaching understanding. And the aim to understand necessarily draws in the universe of meanings by which the researcher him or herself is characterised. Significant problems inhere in attempts to translate interpreted experiences based on the perspective of those studied (first order typifications) into scientific terminology (second order typifications) (Schutz, 1975; Berger and Kellner, 1982). It is these kinds of problems social science inspired by hermeneutics and phenomenology concerns itself with.

In sum, the discovery of the category of meaning leads to an entire set of methodological problems which only serve to add even more contingent factors to scientific knowledge production.

The methodological problems of ethnography and anthropology can be viewed as one long explication of the problems inherent in studying and describing *the Other* (who is a stranger to one's own culture), when the person carrying out the inquiry is unavoidably immersed in the universe of meanings associated with his or her own culture and language (Vidich and Lymann, 2000). At the same time, the fields of ethnography and anthropology explicate how one's perspective impacts on research based understanding: It is only because the researcher's culture differs from the field of study that it is possible to observe anything 'cultural' in it. The entire concept of culture owes its constitution to differences in perspective. When differences in perspective help constitute the object of inquiry, it becomes difficult to image a knowledge production void of contingency.

Signification systems are relative to time and space

The entire sociology of knowledge is a large project which universalises ideas related to those of Marx, Durkheim, and Sapir-Whorf, namely that all signification systems are relative to time and space (Berger and Luckmann, 1979). But sociology of knowledge also contains a clear tightening especially in relation to Marx' notion of false consciousness. Marx was occupied with characterising false consciousness in order to avoid it, whereas sociology of knowledge is concerned with all kinds of knowledge that is taken for granted within a given cultural circle. Thus, sociology of knowledge is more interested in how truth is produced socially and historically, rather than how mistakes are produced (Berger and Luckmann, 1979). Obviously, this kind of approach carries some disturbing implications with it. It is no longer possible to find a location which harbours a trustworthy signification system; the sociology of knowledge will always be able to relativise it to time and space. This goes for science itself.[3]

'Truth' as an institutional product

Foucault has contributed greatly to demonstrating how scientific knowledge production in modern Western societies is closely intertwined with institutional developments; not least institutions occupied with surveying, measuring, diagnosing, differentiating, scrutinising, normalising, and, in the final instance, *creating* human subjects. Having read Foucault, hospitals, schools, prisons, and psychiatric institutions and their related scientific knowledge systems will never be the same again.

Foucault is particularly interested in discourses as a kind of complex and dynamic encounter between scientific epistemes, institutional orders, and practical fields of action (Foucault, 1991; Foucault, 1980; Frank, 1984). Science is fundamentally historical, institutional, and simultaneously producing knowledge and power. Foucault radically constitutes science as part of a societal context. Truth is a product of history and institutions. Science is unavoidably both a product of and a productive power within an institutional space. While truth is being produced within a particular space, the attributes of those subjects acting within the space are also being produced. To put it in another way, one of Foucault's main interests is to show how discursive systems constitute man as a subject (Racevskis, 1983). Notice how controversial this idea is for the core of modern conceptions of science; here the subject was precisely not a product but the starting point for processes of cognition, cf. for example Descartes.

Compared to Marx, Freud, and Durkheim, who put significant but not irreparable question marks to the unmediated consciousness of man, Foucault is taking giant strides in the direction of disarming the notion of a subjective consciousness which is transparent and autonomous. Instead, Foucault demonstrates how this consciousness itself is a discursive product.

Not unlike Foucault, Bourdieu (1977) later demonstrates that not only individual agents, but also the rules for competition and conflict setting them in relation to each other within a given social field, determine the framing

---

3   In order not to complicate matters unnecessarily, Berger and Luckmann keep to discussing every day knowledge in their much cited work on The Social Construction of Reality (1979). However, others have demonstrated how worrying the perspectives for science as such are.

conditions for the practice of science, just like knowledge systems obviously are co-constitutive of certain social fields. The production of knowledge continues to be inseparably bound within its societal context, it becomes a product of socially determined conditions.

The sociology of knowledge makes knowledge relative

A comparable move is made by sociologists of knowledge like Latour (1987), who has studied the actual social circumstances for scientific practice, for example in relation to inventions, laboratory work, and the dissemination of results. A complex configuration of interacting circumstances needs to be in place for the creation of one scientific result above another. Particular definitions of problems are at play, particular constellations of interests and resources, particular networks of persons and institutions showing adequate support for one direction within knowledge production rather than another. It appears that scientific practice departs radically from its own accounts of how it works; science is often much more contingent upon a myriad of micro-contextual factors than it cares to reveal.

One of the main contributions of sociology of knowledge is therefore to turn science itself into an object of scientific inquiry, reflection, and criticism. Thus, science itself contributes to illuminating the contingency of science.

Scientific criticism of science

The thoughts of Latour and the sociologists of knowledge – that science should be an object of study for science – was actually only a premonition of a larger movement which ended up characterising science in modern societies. We have witnessed a long row of enlivening and instructive examples of scientific criticism of so-called scientific 'truths'.

One example is Freeman's (1985) critical revision of Margaret Mead's classic study 'Coming of Age in Samoa' (1973, original pub. 1928). Maybe this classic is a result of a selective choice of sources and Mead's own wishes to articulate a particular contribution to the debate about sexual morality in America to which she was addressing herself, and to which her study possibly only was meant to be an allegoric contribution (for an excellent discussion of possible sources of error, see Maaløe, 1996). Another example is Richard Gillespie's (1991) critical revision of the classic Hawthorne studies, which for decades constituted the original foundation for unquestioned premises about 'human relations' within organisational theory. Gillespie demonstrates how the Hawthorne studies were the results of complex constellations of scientific interests, ideologies, and power relations, which ended up producing what was later to become the well-known and well-established organisational doctrines.

Doubt and reflexivity

The present is also influenced by a continual expansion of scientific doubt to encompass also science itself. This is partly a result of the sociology of knowledge and those traits within philosophy of science that have been promoting doubt for the past 100 years; but it is certainly also a result of reactions prompted by the practical societal effects of science itself. Several of these effects have proved to be rather horrid, ranging from atomic bombs to chemical catastrophes. In this sense, the present is characterised by far too much (scientific) progress, not too little (Beck, 1997). The widespread mood of doubt and criticism in our society focuses on the side effects of progress, technology, bureaucracy, and the market. It is notable how scientific knowledge is drawn into the reflexive and critical work relating to science. Science itself is running the gauntlet in connection with making scientific protest against science (Beck, 1994: 262). Given this state of affairs, it becomes even more difficult for science to emulate the role it was striving for at the beginning of modernity, namely to be as secure, incontrovertible, and authoritative in supplying knowledge as its predecessor carrying the same function: religion.

However, science is not only on the defensive, it is also apt at exploiting its errors as possibilities for expansion (Beck, 1994: 263). A long list of those inconveniences, side effects, and risks which set the agenda in contemporary societies have exactly been mapped, calculated, explicated – in brief constituted – by science itself (Beck, 1994: 265). Problems with methods and results only serve as reasons for more elucidation and research.

Facts only appear today as answers to questions that could have been worded differently (Beck, 1994: 271). If one uses the words 'truth' and 'reality' in scientific circles today, one signals mediocrity and ignorance, Beck notes (1994: 271).

The inherent logic of linguistic presentation

Last, but not least, the contingency of scientific results has appeared in problems related to scientific forms of representation, not least in relation to reporting. In connection with the so-called 'linguistic turn' – that is, a renewed interest in the linguistic character of science – work has been written on how genre, form, and 'tricks' affect results documented in writing (van Maanen, 1988; Clifford and Marcus, 1986; Richardson, 1990).

The written accounts have turned out to be a *display* of that which is represented; it is a way of showing things which set the stage for that which is shown. On top of more general contextual, cultural, institutional, historical, and social contingencies, we now add a particular *rhetorical* contingency to the results of qualitative inquiries. As an epistemological situation, the writing phase is unavoidably influenced by perspectives, it is impossible to write 'from everywhere' but only 'from somewhere' (Richardson, 1990: 27).

A new sensitivity towards problems of representation has appeared, a sensitivity towards how texts pass on an edited and arranged image claiming to represent – display – lived experiences within the field of inquiry. This sensitivity explicates two different trends: (1) a step backwards in hopes for the future possibility of unifying qualitative research results in an overarching Grand Theory, and (2) a step forward for a pursuit of the interest in how local actors produce meaning and these actors' interest in how their voice is subsequently represented in writing. In an interdependent world, it becomes increasingly difficult to isolate and distil authentic cultural differences that can be displayed. At the same time, we have become attuned to details in the rhetorical figures employed by writers of ethnographic works and other types of reports actually employed within qualitative method (Marcus and Fischer, 1986).

The rhetorical effects are expressions of power, culture, history, identity, and relations both within a macro- and micro-perspective. It is through the use of rhetorical effects that the writer establishes a relation to his or her field, for example via reports on scenes of arrival (Pratt, 1986). It is through the use of rhetorical effects that the writer establishes credibility with the reader and establishes him or herself as possessor of authoritative[4] insight at the apex of a hierarchy of understanding (Crapanzano, 1986), for example by overstating his or her lonely trail of cognition, while the dialogic character of the fieldwork is suppressed. It is through the use of rhetorical effects that the writer is able to lay down typifications of actors within the field. Inherent in the typification is a categorisation, a naming, and a selective nomination of those cultural traits that are deemed typical. It is through the use of rhetorical effects that the writer puts forward claims for the truth value of his or her results, and possibly via these also hides and downplays any mistakes that have occurred along the way. It is through the use of rhetorical effects that some actors are given a voice

---

4 The words author and authority possess an interesting common etymology in English. A number of significations are inherent in these words: statement, opinion, citation in support of a point of view, source of citation, decision, power, power to influence thoughts, opinion or behaviour (Webster's Ninth Collegiate Dictionary, 1990).

(and at the same time are selectively 'displayed') within a scientific text, while others are silenced.[5]

It is through the use of rhetorical effects that scientific results are displayed in different ways dependent on the medium and intended readers (Richardson, 1990). And it is through the use of rhetorical effects that it is possible to write about inquiries into one field, while results may be applied allegorically in another field, or even as symbolic of the human condition as such (Clifford, 1986). The rhetoric is a reflection of images of the selected target group which the writer identifies with or aims to persuade, possibly in relation to his or her own development as a human being, or in relation to a given political project.

The attention towards problems of representation has led to an added interest in more open, reflexive, and multi-vocal texts, which simultaneously expose the culture under inquiry and the way of getting to know it (van Maanen, 1988) without essentialising either. There is a comparable interest in types of representation which challenge their own authority (Linstead and Small, 1991: 13), and in 'heterogeneous voices and styles that interact within exclusion' (Jeffcut, 1991: 16). In many instances the wish not to exclude anything – which appears to be a logical impossibility – leads to widespread qualms about even admitting one's authorship.

Contingency in the scientific approach to the empirical

Having shown general trends in the direction of contingency in scientific knowledge production, I now wish to discuss how this principle has impacted on the role that data and the empirical world play in a line of reasoning within the philosophy of science.

Positivism seeks statements that can be securely made on the basis of empirical work. Normative statements and metaphysical speculations are meaningless within a scientific perspective. It is only possible to work in a scientific manner with statements that can be empirically tested. This, however, is at least possible to do ideally through the use of a neutral language of observation and by keeping to a particular set of methodological rules. These rules are above all directions for how to test hypotheses; where the hypotheses originate from and how they are developed are of less concern in this connection. In other words, the positivist notion of secure knowledge obtained through scientific methods is based on a clear distinction between 'context of discovery' and 'context of

---

5 Here we may remind the reader of yet another meaning of the term 'display'; it does not only mean 'show', but also to put something or somebody 'on show' – in effect, the actors are put on the scene to perform or even entertain.

justification' within the scientific process. In the context of discovery, the scientist simply gets a good idea, whose sources cannot be further explicated on the basis of scientific criteria; word has it that Einstein dreamt up the theory of relativity. It is within the context of justification, however, which is empirical, that the methodological rules lead to secure knowledge. The good ideas, the heuristic element, the creative formation of concepts, the almost artistic creation of images of the field of study and its conditions (Nisbet, 1976) – which many scientists regard as a core ingredient in their work – are out of bounds for the application of scientific rules. Only after the hypothesis has been made are the methodological rules applied (Nisbet, 1976).

Positivism is often depicted as a way of thinking oriented towards security – a notion of infallibility and objectivity in the production of knowledge. However, it is also possible in decisive ways to represent it as a kind of thinking which contains seeds of insecurity.

In the perspective of the history of ideas, it is possible to regard positivism as an attempt to counteract the influence of normative dogmas in science. The strategy of positivism is to give primacy to the empirical. This, however, is more difficult than it may sound, because positivism as mentioned above isolates the creative processes from the actual scientific work. This is 'dangerous' for scientific security. To the extent that more than one creative hypothesis may describe a set of empirical phenomena, the floodgates are opened to multiple interpretations. It is only possible to debunk rival hypotheses if one passes a critical empirical test better than another, but a fundamental element of insecurity persists in the fact that even well confirmed hypotheses always may end up being overtaken by equally good hypotheses, as long as there is no scientific control whatsoever with how hypotheses are created.

In addition, the notion of obtaining final verification by following certain methodological rules for hypothesis testing, is a Pandora's Box, which contains something different than expected.

Karl Popper observes that however many empirical observations may fit hypothetical predictions, this will never constitute the final proof of the validity of the hypothesis. One single instance of falsification, however, Popper finds critical. Therefore, he puts forward the notion of falsificationism. Hypotheses have to be expressed in a way that will enable them to be falsified. What characterises a hypothesis (as opposed to a dogma) is that it operates with at least one possibility within empirical findings, which – should it occur – would falsify the hypothesis. Dogmas, on the contrary, remain true irrespective of empirical events. The scientist should concern him or herself with falsifying hypotheses. The more intensely we have worked at falsifying a hypothesis without succeeding, the more we are justified in relying on it. But it is always, by way of principle, subject to potential falsification.

However, empirical events counteracting the predictions of a hypothesis do not always lead to a dismissal of the theory upon which the hypothesis is based. This is expressed in the so-called Duhem-Quine-thesis.

This thesis says that when testing a hypothesis, we are not only testing a single idea, the hypothesis will always be part of a larger network of background assumptions and auxiliary hypotheses. Consequently, it is sometimes unclear whether a critical test result threatens a theory, or whether it threatens a number of less important auxiliary hypotheses. The implications of the Duhem-Quine-thesis are that one is not always able to place responsibility for a falsification on either the core of a theory or its auxiliary conditions (Williams and May, 1996).

Popper demonstrated how the verifications cannot be trusted. Now it appears that the falsifications cannot be trusted either. The undermining of the idea that strict empirical work can lead to secure knowledge becomes increasingly worrisome.

Based on the Duhem-Quine-thesis, it is obvious that falsifications in fact are more rare than would be expected on the basis of Popper's ideas. Lakatos (Williams and May, 1996: 89) touches upon the idea that scientists often stick rather stubbornly with the core of a theory, even if it is empirically under threat. Surrounding the core of a theory there is a zone of auxiliary hypotheses which may be reworked and modified, so that the core of the theory is preserved and maybe even developed further, but not discharged. In this connection, Lakatos expands the perspective to cover not only individual theories, but entire theoretical complexes. He talks about a progressive research program if one is able, over time, to explain an increasing number of phenomena by revising the protective zone surrounding the core of a theory. A degenerative research program, however, does not lead to such advances, in spite of all manner of repair work (Knudsen, 1994: 119).

Thus, a theory is not abandoned on the basis of a single test, but only if scientists through an extended period of time experience it as unproductive, i.e. they suspect that the program will be degenerative. This means that there is an element of 'experience' or 'convention' or 'suspicion' involved in working with theory, and this element is rather resilient to empirical 'falsifications'.

Kuhn represents a more radical version of the same idea.[6] Kuhn operates with the idea that scientific work is organised on the basis of paradigms, which historically, culturally, and institutionally display a certain degree of inertia.

---

6 His theory is approximately 10 years prior to Lakatos', but whereas Lakatos represents a kind of refinement of falsificationism, Kuhn represents a much more fundamental confrontation with it (Knudsen, 1994: 120).

The reasons for keeping a paradigm or – rarer – changing it are often extra-scientific. In addition, observations and methodological rules are dependent on individual paradigms and acquire a different level of acceptability across paradigms. In this way, there is fundamental incommensurability of knowledge generated within two different paradigms (Knudsen, 1994: 121).

Consequently, there is no neutral language of observation. On the contrary, even data is in fundamental ways thoroughly influenced by the point of view, and thereby data becomes contingent in the several ways described in this chapter. To put it another way, knowledge production is both contingent and perspectival. Every time we know something, there is a horizon of assumptions, a perspective, which makes it possible to choose, interpret, and organise information – all of which are compulsory ingredients in knowledge production. But any perspective entails both a loss of taken-for-granteds and an introduction of new taken-for-granteds (Schmidt, 1991: 15).

This section has demonstrated that, if we start from the positivistic idea of secure empirical knowledge, and follow it through the developments of the history of science, we end up being left with social and institutional conventions keeping paradigms together. Only by resolving to a certain set of taken-for-granteds, is it possible to acquire a particular type of new knowledge. Only through one's resolutions is it possible to choose – to an extent – the possible falsifications one may be exposed to. So far in relation to contingency.

However, I will use the following subchapters to maintain that the observation of contingency and perspectivism within knowledge production has to be supplemented with an understanding of rigour.

Rigour

What makes knowledge production a *scientific* activity?

Gellner attempts to delimit scientific activity; he does not take his starting point in formalising particular methodological rules. Gellner leaves these rules inside the 'black box' of science; he starts by noting the societal work carried out by science. This involves a particular kind of societal validation of knowledge. To him, science is connected with an abstract transferral and validation of ideas, which is relatively context-free and de-privatised. In those societies, where science plays a major role, the societal validation of knowledge has been moved from private homes and the church to schools and universities. (University shares its etymological roots with 'the universal', i.e. knowledge which is valid for everyone). In other words, the scientific signals a victory of the trans-social, explicit, formalised, and abstract knowledge above private, unutterable insights or sensitivities (Gellner, 1985: 116). It is this 'style' which lends a colossal productive power to scientific knowledge production. It is this style which, once it has been established, leads to a significant growth in knowledge production, which has had an enormous influence on human systems of production and legitimation (Gellner, 1985: 120).

This scientific 'style' is actually connected with a particular set of values; even if science often presents itself as value-neutral, it is – not necessarily in its specific results, but in its way of working – controlled by values (Bronowski, 1965). Among these values are considerations of clarity and openness for critical discussion.

The thoughts presented above can be recognised in Lars-Henrik Schmidt's summary description of certain traits of scientific activity. As mentioned previously, knowledge production is contingent, because it is perspectival. It always installs a set of taken-for-granteds, while it simultaneously always questions another set of taken-for-granteds; it selects, interprets, and organises. At the same time, knowledge production possesses rigour; it is critical, i.e. capable of inquiring into its own constituting conditions (Schmidt, 1991: 19). Its validity can be tested. It aims to be de-subjectified and de-situationalised, i.e. not be different depending on who expresses it and in which situation. It has a universal aim.

Modern scientific knowledge production carries a historically influenced heritage of believing that something can be true. But in the wake of scientific knowledge production, truth ceases to be something that is revealed. It is not something which suddenly appears. It is no longer an event (Moses receiving the stone tablets), but something that can be produced and reproduced. At the same time, it is gradually acknowledged that the production of truth can be a difficult and elongated process; the contributions to truth along the way may be rather partial, temporary, and fragile; and maybe truth is only an ideal, which should never be confused with any concrete statement (Schmidt, 1991: 14).

This gradual and laborious work, which presupposes an ideal about truth for which we will never be able to take out a final patent, is characterised by a number of things that are central to the definition of what it means to be scientific: these include a well articulated conceptual delimitation, clarity in operationalising concepts, and diligent observations that are handled using publicly accessible methods (Gellner, 1985: 126).

It becomes clear how the explicated, de-privatised, and externalised account of the starting point for knowledge production and ongoing work – which is open to critical testing – makes a significant contribution to the definition of science.

Richard Rorty has, from a philosophical starting point, contributed to undermine the notion of absolute and irrefutable knowledge. Instead, he characterises truth as 'what our peers will let us get away with saying' (Rorty, quoted in Tarnas, 1996: 399).

This, however, is not as simple as it may sound. Those 'peers' are socially and historically rooted in a type of society which among its heritage can count a certain belief in rational knowledge production. When we consider the strong impact the notion of true, rigorous, explicit, formal, and critically tested knowledge has had on the institutions of modern society, the implications of Rorty's statement become anything but lax. He is right in observing that the foundational conditions of scientific knowledge are contingent. But these contingent conditions are dependent on social history in a way that is not superficial at all. Institutions, rules, and practices are in place which contributes to giving science a place to be explicit, public, and external. 'What our peers will let us get away with saying' is not entirely random.

Castoriadis claims that reason is a crucial principle for controlling knowledge in modern societies because of the discovery of the autonomy inherent in social organisation. 'To be accountable more precisely implies that we will explain to ourselves whether something is true or not, [...] by lending it consideration – and not by reading the Bible, the Koran, or a story about Buddha's life, etc. I for one, or all of us, or the general public, will not accept a particular rule without discussion, just because it has been passed on from our ancestors or because it is recognised or possesses authority; the general public wants to know why they should accept the rule, and here the discussion starts. To discuss something, it is necessary to jointly agree on certain rules that cannot be proven'. In modern societies, these preconditions are attached to reason. 'This implies that the standpoint of reason in itself cannot be motivated. [...] We do not believe that reason is insane or arbitrary, because from the moment we accept responsibility, a controllable development starts, a development which may not be controlled using mathematical instruments, but social historical ones' (Castoriadis, interview in Rötzer, 1987: 53) The possibility of cultivating a more or less rational, critical discourse is dependent on a particular type of community (Douglas, 1986 b: 84), which is a social historical construction, even a quite unique social construction. When science is placed in the world on the basis of the principle of contingency, it is simultaneously necessary to apply rigour, ie. science is contingent upon a particular status, an institutional affiliation, and last but not least, its own mechanisms of self-regulation.

Longino (2002) carried out a thorough philosophical reading of the insistence by modern sociology of knowledge that all knowledge is contingent, and culturally and socially determined. Her answer, however, is that any opposition between 'social' and 'rational' types of knowledge is artificial and misleading. To recognise that knowledge production is social, context- bound, and secular is not the same as dismissing the possibility of letting it regulate matters in a tolerably rational way.

Therefore, the discovery that the scientific is defined by social rules does not have to lead to endless loops of contingency, because it is implied by the social historic contingent conditions for modern science, that they in themselves lend a certain degree of institutional protection to scientific activity that is external, de-privatised, and subjected to critical discussion. Rigour implies a remarkable type of *fearlessness*: the researcher persists in the clarity and consequence of his/her methodological logic, irrespective of those costs it may have in terms of preferred values and practical persecutions. Via the valorisation of reason in modern society, we can even, to a certain degree, talk about an institutionally protected fearlessness (which, however, naturally is in continual confrontation with other institutional concerns, principles, values, and interests).

Why is it that the discovery of the contingency of knowledge production, which is described above from the discovery of the constitutive role of language for cognition, and realisation of the perspectival character of all knowledge, to Foucault's debunking of the confidence of modern science, why has all of this appeared as giant gains for cognition, while at the same time providing any student with a minimum of theoretical interest in science with butterflies in their stomachs? It is because all this has to be understood in close relation to the context which provides valorisation of the modern, externalised, rationally controlled, and simultaneously truth-seeking and critical scientific effort. It is through its contrast with attempts to de-subjectify knowledge that the discovery of the subjectivity of knowledge gains significance; it is through its contrast with efforts towards acquiring certainty of knowledge that the emphasis on the insecurity of all knowledge becomes particularly interesting. Detached from this context, the discovery of contingency within the production of knowledge may appear incoherent and lead to bizarre consequences. This is what happens when students read a few pages by Foucault and decide to establish a consultancy firm based on a philosophy of 'knowledge is power'.

Rigour in analysing meaning

It may be claimed that an explicit, formal, externalised, and relatively de-subjectified knowledge production would be more difficult, or even downright impossible, when the field of study is constituted by socially defined meaning structures. In a given social situation, an act is illuminated from within by the meaning the actor confers upon it (Berger, 1970). Any scientific occupation with this has to be based on an understanding, an interpretive way of encountering the perspective of the actor. This is difficult, among other things because every constellation of meaning possesses its own ideographic traits – it differs from context to context. At the same time, the word 'context' says nothing in itself, it only refers to 'everything surrounding a given situation' that may be of consequence for understanding the situation (Mishler, 1979). Providing a given social situation with meaning can be complex; there will always be a possibility of multiple identities, multiple frames of interpretation, multiple institutional relations and rules, all of which may be brought into play contextually.

This means that it is necessary to take a kind of 'holistic' perspective on the field of study, at least until one has obtained a better understanding of those attributes of the context which lend meaning to the text (the act under inquiry, patterns of action, etc.). In other words, it is possible to call upon arguments about meaning, ideography, holism, and complexity (possibly in interplay with each other) when one has to argue for the particular difficulties of studying social/human phenomena.

In addition, there is an argument about subjectivity. It is up for interpretation which factors within a context are meaningful and relevant; the interpreter him or herself is a subject. The interpretation depends on the interpreter's aim to understand, and even will to provide an interpretation; without this willingness there will be no understanding. Above, I touched upon the radical contingency and perspectivism attached to the interpretation of constellations of meaning.

This, however, does not rule out the possibility of testing in an explicit, externalised, and critically testable way. Both hermeneutics and phenomenologists have consciously and systematically worked on what it means to be rigorous when interpreting constellations of meaning. Within hermeneutics, Ricoeur has worked with the concept of *text*, which already possesses a certain degree of externality in its data material in comparison with a purely internal intentionality.

Phenomenologists operate with a *phenomenological reduction*, whereby they attempt to describe things anew in order to be able to be surprised about the world (Merleau-Ponty, 1962), and where they do not claim to describe things as they are, but only as they appear (Giorgi, 1988: 172). The theory of phenomenological reduction is that all our conceptual fixations are oriented by our actual engagement with the world (Merleau-Ponty, 1962). This engagement informs particular structures of relevance for our typifications of those phenomena that appear real to our consciousness (Schutz, 1975). It does, however, lie within the power of our consciousness to bracket our assumptions and seek to regard the world anew, just like we posses the ability to order our conceptual orientations according to *another, non-practical structure of relevance, namely a theoretical one* (Berger and Kellner, 1982). In the light of theoretical considerations, we are capable, on the basis of our understanding of the 1st order typifications of stakeholders themselves, to construct theoretically relevant 2nd order typifications (Berger and Kellner, 1981) which all posses a relative level of generality.

It may be discussed whether the externality inherent in for example Riceour's concept of text may be extended to also hold good for the content of meaning in human actions. It may be that what reduction teaches us above all, is that a total reduction is impossible (Merleau-Ponty, 1962). And it may be that a theoretical structure of relevance never is completely isolated from the rest of the world. Even a theoretical relevance structure is contingent.

Nevertheless, phenomenology and hermeneutics have contributed considerably to deliver principles of interpretation that are both rather externalised and critically reflexive. The fact that social and cultural studies are occupied with studying constellations of meaning, does not disable them from producing explicit and critically testable knowledge. If science is regarded as part of human interpretative work (Cassirer, 1946), rather than regarding interpretation as a part of science, it becomes obvious that a number of scientific problems are rather common, as opposed to being especially damning for those parts of science occupied with society and culture, in brief, with socially defined structures of meaning.

The connection between contingency and rigour

The principles of contingency and rigour are often posed against each other. Either knowledge is absolute or relative. Either it is subjective or objective. Either it is secure or insecure. Proponents of particular schools, traditions, and views have often cultivated one principle above the other, often adding to the conflict between the two.

A number of interesting scientific theoretical contributions, however, aim to demonstrate that these principles are connected by a number of fine threads; they are complementary and mutually dependent on different levels. It is possible to conceive of a connection between attempts to pull science in the direction of contingency and, ultimately, deconstruction, and attempts towards integration and reconciliation (Tarnas, 1996: 407).

The idea that there is bias in a given viewpoint is often based on the unrealistic ideal of an absolute and flawless viewpoint (Merleau-Ponty, 1962). Merleau-Ponty operates with the idea that the truth to which we have access is reached not in spite of our historical position, but because of it.

In other words, it is the instalment of perspective, including the instalment of certain taken-for-granteds, which facilitates an insight into everything that the perspective renders not evident.[7]

The knowing subject is not capable of accounting for all the conditions constituting that person's knowledge perspective. Bateson (1972) already demonstrated that the monitoring part of a system is incapable of monitoring the entire system. There is something fundamentally unfinished about scientific understanding, it is incapable of demonstrating the premises on which its premises are based in perpetuity.

But it is possible to appreciate the unfinished character of scientific work (Bouchet, 1990: 45). The subject, which is not sovereign and omniscient, but which is contingent, inadequate, wavering, humble, and mortal (Bouchet, 1990: 37) is actually capable of subjecting its own knowledge to reflection. This possibility is furthered even more as the idea of incontrovertible truth becomes increasingly untenable. It is possible to connect knowledge of the world with knowledge of the knowing spirit, and vice versa (Morin, 1990: 212). It is possible to reflect upon the constituting conditions for one's perspective, it is even an ingredient in the definition of science itself, even if these reflections encounter limitations, and not all preconditions can be reflected upon. In brief, it is possible to practice *active perspectivism* (Schmidt, quoted in Pedersen and Larsen, 1995: 52).

Active perspectivism

This is a kind of perspectivism that takes an active stand in relation to its own constituting conditions – both the constitution of the perspective and the constitution of the field of study at the same time.

Active perspectivism is the opposite of passive perspectivism, where one does not admit to the significance of the perspective in installing taken-for-granteds via the constitution of the field of study. Passive perspectivism can sometimes be found in student projects where 'the choice of theory' has been discussed in the sense of 'some kind of theoretical approach that fits the part of reality I have chosen as my object of study'. Passive perspectivism is also common with students and researchers who work with several perspectives within the same project.

---

7 The pleasure of playing a game of chess is dependent upon, on the one hand, the many possibilities for moving the pieces on the board, and on the other hand, those rules constitution the game of chess as a game. If a move with the bishop (only diagonally!) unconditionally could be changed by a move with innumerable other pieces, or shots from a machine gun, or something completely different, it would be impossible to be fascinated by the game of chess.

Martin (1992), for example claims that, if one applies three different perspectives on an organisational culture, one gains a more complete understanding than if only applying one. When using such multiple perspectives in approaching a field of study, the researcher often ends up simplifying each perspective to highlight the interplay between them as far as possible (they isolate and simplify for example 'the rational' and 'the sociological' institutionalism in ways that make adherents of either unable to recognise or endorse the presentation of their 'own' perspective). A further risk with this kind of perspectivism, where several approaches are applied in the same project – which is very common in organisational theory – is that the perspective from which one assesses and synthesises the selected perspectives is not discussed. Martin (1992) does not, for example, at all discuss what a fourth perspective or a meta-perspective may even look like, if they are at all capable of amalgamating such a more 'complete understanding'. As readers, we are left in doubt about whether it is even the same object that is being described.

Active perspectivism, on the other hand, is conscious of the fact that we do not just 'talk about the same' when the perspective changes. Active perspectivism takes account of its constituting conditions, and is simultaneously both contingent and rigorous.

Contingent rigour and rigorous contingency

Active perspectivism makes two methodological principles interact, namely contingency and rigour at both subordinate and superior levels within the methodological work. In figure 5.1, these levels are called micro- and macro-level. They are defined relatively rather than in absolute terms. For example, the paradigmatic level is 'macro' in relation to the methodological level which is 'micro', but in relation to concrete questioning techniques at 'micro-level', the methodological design is 'macro'.

Figure 5.1

Contingency at macro-level	Rigour at macro-level
Contingency at micro-level	Rigour at micro-level

Active perspectivism makes the two levels and the two principles interact with each other. If one rigorously keeps to one paradigm at macro-level, it is still healthy to account for the contingent constituting conditions of this paradigm (for example its place within the history of ideas). If working rigorously with a paradigm, it is healthy to relate to the contingent nature of methodological possibilities within it (the paradigm renders some methods reasonable and others not). But if a particular methodological approach has been chosen, it should be rigorously applied. Rigorous method at micro-level can be the best medicine to ensure that no phenomena calling for a revision of one's prior conceptual understandings are overlooked.

This means that active perspectivism makes use of available methodological possibilities for critical validation. Active perspectivism not only aims to reflect its contingency in relation to that which is 'outside' of its perspective; it also aims to demonstrate its usefulness and limitations via rigorous application 'inside' the perspective.

There is potential in being inspired by Popper here. By keeping within one's perspective, but at the same time following it rigorously to its limits and perhaps to the point of falsification, you arrive at the clearest possible delimitation of it, and find out how useful it is.

Any way of thinking is taking its risks (Morin, 1990: 222). One of the risks an inquiry runs is that it empirically will lead to something different than expected. This means that perspectivism is not only a reproduction of that which is already known. Perspectivism is to run the risk of installing a certain set of taken-for-granteds and dismantling another set at the same time. Active perspectivism demonstrates the abilities of the perspective, and in carrying out this demonstration, it is my claim that making displays in accordance with the rules of authenticity, inclusion, and transparency can contribute productively to a concrete analysis.

When working with displays, one attempts to work as rigorously as possible at the micro-level of data, while at the same time recognising a larger contingency in each of the methodological steps. It is not opposed to, but may actually be entirely consistent with, the conscious recognition that an inquiry also at macro-level is both contingent and rigorous.

Summary

> *It is my contention – superstition if you like – that he who is faithful to his map, and consults it, and draws from it his inspiration, daily and hourly, gains positive support… The tale has a root here: it grows in that soil; it has a spine of its own behind the words… As he studies the map, relations will appear that he had not thought upon.*
>
> Robert L. Stevenson[1]

> *It seems, in fact, that you do not truly begin to think until you attempt to lay out your ideas and information … you are never truly inside a topic – or on top of it – until you face the hard task of explaining it to someone else.*
>
> Lofland and Lofland

A display is a table or other form of graphic presentation of qualitative data in a concentrated form. The display does not present a convenient selection of data or a particularly telling example. The display is constructed to present a complete set of data in one place, simultaneously facilitating an answer to the research question (Miles and Huberman, 1994: 188).

I have suggested that displays should be made according to the rules of authenticity, inclusion, and transparency. Obviously, neither the use of displays nor these three rules are panacea. They can only be meaningfully applied when their mechanical character is combined with the content and interpretive aspects of an inquiry.

But displays often turn out to have a number of beneficial effects in relation to qualitative inquiries. For the reader of a report the following may apply:

---

[1] Stevenson is the author of Treasure Island and quoted in Harvey (2000: 39).

- A display shows a way of prioritising; this may be an important major result.

- The display sorts through, prioritises, and not least condenses a large amount of data, making it visible in a limited space.

- A display relates clearly to theory by virtue of the fact that its axes and main components are theoretical concepts or bridge building concepts which clearly refer back to theory.

- A display relates clearly to data by containing bridge building concepts whose empirical expressions are clearly visible.

- The display shows how data leads to the conclusions that are made. The display helps pull data into answering the research questions that have been posed.

For these reasons, the display is an excellent means of communication between the reader and the researcher. The display is a way of crystallising everything the researcher wants to tell the reader.

Figure 6.1 Modes of expression for inquiries:

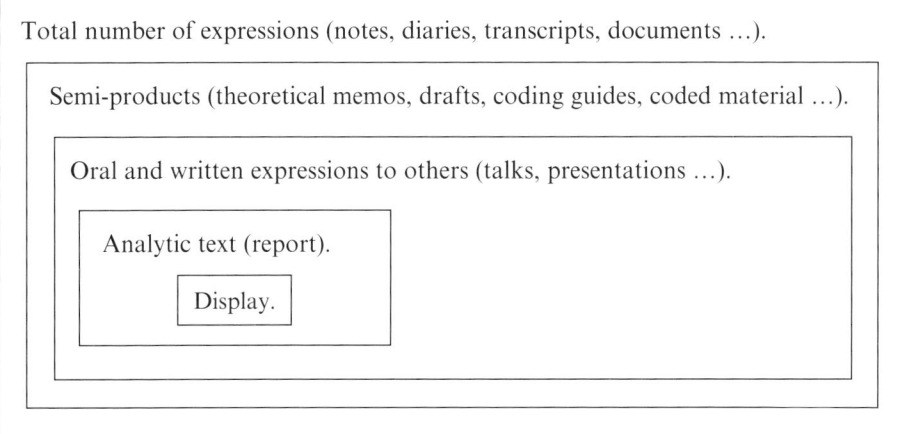

The display is a result of – and dependent upon – many of the other ways of expression. But at the same time, it is a means of communication that both the report writer and the reader share and focus most intensely on. It is precisely an expression of the prioritised and condensed message that both relate to. When

Summary   113

having to tell others about one's own qualitative inquiry, one often has far too great expectations to how much time and attention others set aside to receive the message. One often has to be content with being able to produce *one* good display that the others relate to and remember. This may be a relevant aim for a qualitative inquiry and a way of providing meaning to one's life!

But a display also functions in a number of excellent ways during an inquiry. Making a good display may be closely intertwined with living up to standards of validity and good craftsmanship in a qualitative inquiry. The researcher may experience any of the following:

- The display can help prioritise and pinpoint what is central to the inquiry.

- The display can help delimit the research field one is making statements about. When data is limited in this way (is *bounded*), it becomes easier to reach *saturation* point (Glaser and Strauss, 1967), and thus draw conclusions about data.

- The display can help concentrate large amounts of data and store them.

- The display can help identify both gaps and anomalies in data.

- The way the display juxtaposes data leads to inference. Conclusions can be made once data starts interacting with itself.

- The display can be used for communicative validation.

- The display can make the connection between data and conclusion transparent.

- In sum, the display makes it possible to deduct, argue for, and maintain the main analytic point of an inquiry.

Obviously, no guarantees are given. One of the negative side effects of a display may be that at an early stage it ends up working as a Procrustean bed that data is forcefully fitted into, and that there is too much focus on the mechanical aspects rather than the epistemological aspects of an inquiry. This is determined more by how the researcher uses the display than by the display as such. But of course, the disadvantages need to be weighed against the advantages.

Above all, the most substantial and common function of the display is that it works as a trigger for the researcher to pull together, concentrate, and explicate what he or she believes to know. This may be epistemologically fruitful. 'How can I know what I write until I see what I think?,' we usually say to ourselves when we have to present something. But using a paraphrase of the American organisational researcher Karl Weick, we may equally well ask, 'How can I know what I think until I see what I write?'.

In this sense, a display may serve a remarkable auto-communicative function, just like writing letters, which through its *externalisation* of a description also becomes a way of self-reflection.

Thus, the display may function as a triple conglomerate of the inquiry's internal representation of an external reality, of the possibility of the inquiry for studying this presentation anew, and of the possibility of the reader to study both. And maybe remember the main message of the qualitative inquiry for a while.

Whether contemporary displays from qualitative inquiries are likely to catch the attention of readers in 200 years' time, in the same way that my attention was caught by the image of the grand chief of the Iroquois, seems unlikely. Maybe our displays will be less colourful, exotic, and grand than the handsome Iroquois. But maybe our displays may, to a greater extent than the image of the Iroquois, be disciplined by rules for how we display what we see.

References

Alasuutari, Pertti (1995): *Researching Culture*. London – Thousand Oaks: Sage Publications.

Asad, T (1986): "The Concept of Cultural Translation in British Social Anthropology", in *Writing Culture*, J. M. Clifford & G. E. Marcus (eds.) Berkeley: University of California Press.

Bateson, Gregory (1972): *Steps to an Ecology of Mind.* New York: Ballantine Books.

Beck, Ulrich (1997): *Risikosamfundet – på vej mod en ny modernitet.* [Risk Society – Towards a New Modernity] Copenhagen: Hans Reitzels Forlag.

Beck, Ulrich (1994): "The Reinvention of Politics: Towards a Theory of Reflexive Modernization", in *Reflexive Modernization*, Ulrich Beck, Anthony Giddens & Scott Lash (eds.). Stanford: Stanford University Press.

Berger, Peter L. &Thomas Luckmann (1979): *Den Samfundsskabte Virkelighed.* [The Social Construction of Reality: A Treatise in the Sociology of Knowledge] Copenhagen: Lindhardt & Ringhof.

Berger, Peter L. (1970): "Identity As a Problem in the Sociology of Knowledge", in *The Sociology of Knowledge. A Reader*, P. Curtis (ed.). New York: Praeger.

Berger, Peter L. & Hansfried. Kellner (1982): *Nytolkning af Sociologien: et essay om metode og engagement.* [Sociology Reinterpreted: An Essay on Method and Vocation] Ålborg: Lindhardt og Ringhof.

Bouchet, Dominique (1990): "En metode der respekterer det komplekse", [A Method for Respecting Complexity] in *Kendskabet til kundskaben, en erkendelsens antropologi*, Edgar Morin (ed.) Århus: Forlaget Ask, 5-19-237-238.

Bourdieu, Pierre (1977): *Outline of a Theory of Practice*. Cambridge University Press.

Bronowski, J. (1965): *Science and Human Values.* New York: Harper & Row.

Cassirer, E. (1965): *Et essay om mennesket.* [Essay on Man] Copenhagen: Munksgård.

Cassirer, E. (1946): *Language and Myth.* New York: Dover Publications.

Castoriadis, C. (1987): "Det Imaginære: Skabelsen i det Social-historiske Felt", *Paradigma,* 2 (1), 15-28.

Clifford, J. & G. Marcus (1986): *Writing Culture. The Poetics and Politics of Ethnography*. Berkeley: University of California Press.

Clifford, James (1986): "On Ethnographic Allegory", in *Writing Culture. The Poetics and Politics of Ethnography*, James Clifford & George E. Marcus (eds.). Berkeley: University of California Press, 98-121.

Crapanzano, V. (1986): "Hermes' Dilemma: The Masking of Subversion in Ethnographic Description", in *Writing Culture. The Poetics and Politics of Ethnography*, James Clifford & George E. Marcus (eds.). Berkeley: University of California Press.

Dahler-Larsen, Peter (1993): *Fællesskabet af dem, som intet fællesskab har. En sociologisk undersøgelse af organisationskultur hinsides et integrationsperspektiv*. Odense: Odense Universitetsforlag.

Dahler-Larsen, Peter (1997): "Organizational Identity as a "Crowded Category": A Case of Multiple and Quickly Shifting We-typifications", in *Cultural Complexity in Organizations: Contrasts and Contradictions*, S. Sackmann, (ed.). Thousand Oaks: Sage.

Denzin, Norman K. & Yvonna S. Lincoln (2000): *Handbook of Qualitative Research*. Thousand Oaks: Sage.

Denzin, Norman K. (2000): "The Practices and Politics of Interpretation", in *Handbook of Qualitative Research*, Norman K. Denzin & Yvonna S. Lincoln (eds.). Thousand Oaks, California: Sage, 897-922.

Douglas, M. (1986): *How Institutions Think*. London: Routledge.& Keagan Paul.

Douglas, M. (1986b): "The Social Preconditions of Radical Scepticism", in *Power, Action, and Belief: A New Sociology of Knowledge?*, J. Law (ed.) London: Routledge & Keagan Paul.

Eco, Umberto (1998): *Serendipities. Language and Lunacy*. New York: Columbia University Press.

ECRI (2006): *Third Report on Denmark*. Strasbourg: Council of Europe.

Edström, Anders, Lars E. Norbäck, & J. E. Rendahl (1989): *Förnyelsens ledarskap. SAS' utveckling från flybolag til reiseforetag*. Stockholm: Norstedt.

Engels, Friedrich (1884/1970): *The Origins of the Family, Private Property and the State*. New York: International Publishers.

Fink, Anne S. (2000): "Kvalitative data i Dansk Data Arkiv," *Metode & Data*, 83 – 2000, 3-17.

Fontana, Andrea & James H. Frey (1994): "Interviewing: The Art of Science", in *Handbook of Qualitative Research*, Norman K. Denzin & Yvonna S. Lincoln (eds.) Thousand Oaks: Sage, 361-76.

Foucault, M. (1980): "Power/Knowledge", in *Selected Interviews and Other Writings 1972-77 by Michel Foucault*, Colin Gordon (ed.). New York: Harvester.

Foucault, M. (1991): "The Foucault Effect. Studies in Governmentality. With two lectures by and an Interview with Michel Foucault.", Graham Burchell, Colin Gordon, & Peter Miller (eds.) London: Harvester.

Frank, Victor E. (1984): *Man's Search for Meaning*. New York: Washington Square Press.

Freeman, F. H. (1985): "Books That Mean Business", *Academy of Management Review,* 10, April, 345-50.

Geertz, C. (1975): *The Interpretation of Cultures. Selected Essays.* London: Hutchinson.

Gellner, Ernest (1985): *Relativism and the Social Sciences.* Cambridge: Cambridge University Press.

Gibbons, M., C. Limoges, H. Nowotny, S. Schwartzman, P. Scott, & M. Trow (1994): *The New Production of Knowledge. The Dynamics of Science and Research in Contemporary Societies.* London: Sage.

Gillespie, Richard (1991): *Manufacturing Knowledge. A history of the Hawthorne Experiments.* New York, Port Chester: Cambridge University Press.

Giorgi, A. (1988): "Validity and Reliability from a Phenomenological Perspective", in *Recent Trends in Theoretical Psychology*, W. J. Baker (ed.). New York: Springer-Verlag.

Glaser, Barney G. & Anselm L. Strauss (1967): *The Discovery of Grounded Theory.* Chicago: Aldine.

Guba, Egon G. & Yvonna S. Lincoln (1989): *Fourth Generation Evaluation.* Newbury Park: Sage.

Hammersley, M. & Paul Atkinson (1987): *Feltmetodikk. [Ethnography, Principles in Practice].* Oslo: Gyldendal Norsk Forlag.

Hansen, Thorkild (1964): *Arabia Felix: The Danish Expedition of 1761-1767.* New York: Harper & Row

Harvey, Miles (2000): *The Island of Lost Maps. A True Story of Cartographic Crime.* New York: Broadway Books.

Jacob, F. (1985): *Mulighedernes spil* – om det levendes mangfoldighed [Le Jeu des Possibles: Essai sur la Diversité du Vivant]. Copenhagen: Hekla.

Jeffcutt, Paul (1991): *Styles of Representation in Organizational Analysis.* Paper submitted to the 8.SCOS-conference, Copenhagen, 28 – 30 juni, 1991.

Jones, G. R. (1983): "Life History Methodology", in *Beyond Method: Strategies for Social Research*, G. E. Morgan (ed.). Beverly Hills: Sage, 147-59.

Kjelbo, Ib (1966): *Historisk kartografi.* Copenhagen: Dansk Historisk Fællesforenings Håndbøger.

King, G, R. O. Keohane & S. Verba (1994): *Designing Social Inquiry.* Princeton: Princeton University Press.

Kjærsgaard, Sten W. (1991): *Columbus'hemmelige dagbog.* Kolding: Branner og Korch.

Kneer, Georg and Armin Nassehi (1993): *Niklas Luhmanns Theorie sozialer Systeme: eine Einführung*. München: Fink.
Knudsen, Christian (1994): "Empirisk-analytisk videnskabsteori. Del 1: Induktivismen og dens kritikere", in *Introduktion. Videnskabsteori & metodelære*, Heine Andersen (ed.) Copenhagen: Samfundslitteratur, 101-21.
Knudsen (1999): ""Noble Savages" a review of Harry Liberson (1998)" *Weekendavisen*, 8-14 October, 1999.
Kvale, Steinar (1996): *InterViews*. Thousand Oaks: Sage.
Langer, Susanne K. (1957): *Philosophy in a New Key*. Cambridge: Harvard University Press.
Latour, Bruno (1987): *Science in Action. How to Follow Scientists and Engineers through Society*. Stony Stratford: Open University Press.
Latour, Bruno (1996): *Vi har aldri vært moderne. Essay i symmetrisk antropologi*. Oslo: Spartacus forlagas.
Liebersohn, Harry (1998): *Aristocratic Encounters. European Travelers and North American Indians*. Cambridge: Cambridge University Press.
Lijphardt, A (1971): "Comparative Politics and the Comparative Method", *American Political Science Review*, LXV.
Linstead, S & Robert C. Small (1991): *No Visible Means of Support: Ethnography and the end of Deconstruction*. Paper presented at the 8. SCOS-conference in Copenhagen, 28-30. juni, 1991.
Longio, Helen E. (2002): *The Fate of Knowledge*. Princeton: Princeton University Press.
Luckmann, Thomas (1978): "Philosophy, Social Sciences and Everyday Life", in *Phenomenology and Sociology*, Thomas Luckmann (ed.). Harmondsworth: Penguin, 217-53.
Maaløe, Erik (1996): *Case-studier af og om mennesker i organisationer*. Copenhagen: Akademisk Forlag.
Manata, Hanne, Morten E. Petersen & Per Østergaard (1991): *AIDS. Prostitution og Kommunikation*. Odense: Fyns Amt.
Marcus, George E. & Michael M. J. Fisher (1986): *Anthropology as Cultural Critique*. Chicago: The University of Chicago Press.
Martin, J. (1992): *Cultures in Organizations. Three Perspectives*. New York: Oxford University Press.
Maxwell, Joseph A. (1996): *Qualitative Research Design. An Interactive Approach*. Thousand Oaks, California: Sage.
Mead, Margaret (1973): *Coming of Age in Samoa*. New York: Morrow.
Merleau-Ponty, M. (1962): *Phenomenology of Perception*. London: Routledge.
Merleau-Ponty, M. (1969): *Tegn. Udvalgte Essays*. [Signs] København: Rhodos.

Merleau-Ponty, M. (1978): "The Philosopher and Sociology", in *Phenomenology and Sociology*, Thomas Luckmann, (ed.) Middlesex: Penguin Books, 142-60.
Meyerson, Debra (1991): ""Normal" Ambiguity?: A Glimpse of an Occupational Culture", in *Reframing Organizational Cultures*, P. M. Frost & et al. (eds.). Newsbury Park: Sage.
Miles, Matthew B. & A. M. Hubermann (1994): *Qualitative Data Analysis*. London: Sage.
Mirvis, PH. (1985): "Managing Research while Researching Managers", in *Organizational Culture*, Peter J. Frost & et al. (eds.). Beverly Hills: Sage, 201-22.
Mishler, E. G. (1979): "Meaning in Context: Is there any other kind?", *Harvard Educational Review*, 49 1-19.
Morin, Edgar (1981): "Can We Conceive of a Science of Autonomy?", *Cahiers Internationaux de Sociologie*, LXXI 257-67.
Morin, Edgar (1990): *Kendskabet til Kundskaben. En erkendelsens antropologi.* [La Méthode: la Connaissance de la Connaissance: Anthropologie de la Connaissance] Århus: Ask.
Nisbet, R (1976): *Sociology as an Art Form*. London: Heinemann.
Nisbet, R. (1980): *History of the Idea of Progress*. New York: Basic Books.
Nisbet, Robert (1966): *The Sociological Tradition*. London: Heinemann.
Oreszczyn S. & Lane A. (2000): "The Meaning of Hedgerows in the English Landscape: Different Stakeholder Perspectives and the Implications for Future Hedge Management", *Journal of Environmental Management*, 60 (1),101-18.
Oxford Advanced Learner's Dictionary (2000) Sixth edition. Oxford: Oxford University Press. (First Published in 1948).
Padilla, Raymond V. (1994): "The Unfolding Matrix: A Technique for Qualitative Data Acoquisition and Analysis", *Studies in Qualitative Methodology*, 4, 273-85.
Pedersen, P. P. & Stenback Larsen (1995): "Ingen vil være sociologer. Interview med Lars-Henrik Schmidt", *Tendens*, 7 (2), 37-55.
Politiken (2001): "Diskrimination: Rapport fra Den Europæiske Kommission mod Racisme og Intolerance" (ECRI). 04.04.2001, p. 2.
Pratt, M. (1986): "Fieldwork in Common Places", in *Writing Culture*, James Clifford & George E. Marcus (eds.). Berkeley: University of California Press, 27-50.
Psathas, G. E. (1973): *Phenomenological Sociology*. New York: John Wiley and Sons.
Racevskis, Karelis (1983): *Michel Foucault and the Subversion of Intellect*. Ithaca, New York: Cornell University Press.

Ragin (1994): *Constructing Social Research: the Unity and Diversity of Method.* Thousand Oaks: Pine Forge Press.
Richardson, Laurel (1990): *Writing Strategies. Reaching Diverse Audiences.* Newbury Park – London: Sage Publications.
Richardson, Laurel (2000): "Writing: A Method of Inquiry", in *Handbook of Qualitative Research*, Norman K. Denzin & Yvonna S. Lincoln (eds.). Thousand Oaks, California: Sage, 923-48.
Rötzer, Florian (1987): "Cornelius Castoriadis", in *Samtaler med Franske Filosoffer.* [Conversations with French Philosophers] Copenhagen: Akademisk Forlag, 45-62.
Saussure, F. d. (1959): *A Course in General Linguistics.* New York: McGraw-Hill Book Company.
Schatzmann, L.S. & A. Strauss (1973): *Field Research.* Englewood Cliffs, NJ: Prentice-Hall.
Schmidt, L-H. (1991): *Det Videnskabelige Perspektiv.* Viborg: Akademisk Forlag.
Schmidt, Lars-Henrik (2000): Det Sociale Selv. Invitation til Socialanalytik. København: Danmarks Pædagogiske Institut.
Schutz, Alfred (1975): *Hverdagslivets Sociologi.* Copenhagen: Hans Reitzels Forlag.
Schwandt, Thomas A. (2002): *Evaluation Practice Reconsidered.* New York: Peter Lang.
Schwandt, Thomas A. (2006): "Opposition Redirected", *International journal of Qualitative Studies in Education*, 19 (6), 803-810.
Schwandt, Thomas A. (2000): "Three Epistemological Stances for Qualitative Inquiry: Interpretevism, Hermeneutics, and Social Constructivism", in *Handbook of Qualitative Research*, Norman K. Denzin & Yvonna S. Lincoln (eds.). Thousand Oaks: Sage, 189-214.
Scott, Dianne & Cathy Oelofse (2007): "The Staging of Public Participation in Envirimental Policy Processes: The Point Small Craft Harbour in Durban, South Africa", *Draft.* University of KwaZulu-Natal, South Africa.
Smircich, L. (1983): "Organizations as Shared Meanings", in *Organizational Symbolism*, L. R. Pondy (ed.). Greenwich: JAI Press.
Tarnas, R (1996): *The Passion of the Western Mind. Understanding the Ideas That Have Shaped Our World View.* New York: Harmony Books.
Tocqueville, A. (1978): *Lighed og Frihed. Uddrag fra "Demokratiet i Amerika".* [Democracy in America] Haarby: Forlaget i Haarby.
Turner, B. (1971): *Exploring the Industrial Subculture.* London: MacMillan.
van Maanen, J. & S. Barley (1984): "Occupational Communities: Culture and Control in Organizations", in *Research in Organizational Behaviour, vol. 6*, L. L. S. Cummings, (ed). Greenwich: JAI Press.

van Maanen, J. (1988): *Tales of the Field. On writing Ethnography*. Chicago: University of Chicago Press.
Vidich, Arthur J. & Stanford M. Lyman (2000): "Qualitative Methods: Their History in Sociology and Anthropology", in *Handbook of Qualitative Research*, Norman K. Denzin & Yvonna S. Lincoln, (eds.). Thousand Oaks: Sage, 37-84.
Wax, Rosalie (1971): *Doing Fieldwork*. Chicago: The University of Chicago Press.
Weber, Max (1946): *From Max Weber: Essays in Sociology*. New York: Oxford University Press.
Webster's Ninth New Collegiate Dictionary. (1990) Springfield: Merriam-Webster Inc.
Webster's Encyclopaedic Unabridged Dictionary of the English language (1996) New York: Gramercy Books.
Weick, Karl E. (1979): "Cognitive Processes in Organizations", in *Research in Organizational Behaviour, vol 1*, L. Staw (ed.). Greenwich: JAI Press, 41-74.
Williams, Malcolm & Tim May (1996): *Introduction to the Philosophy of Social Research*. London: Routledge.
Winsløw, Jacob H. (1991): "Sociologisk Forulempning", *Social Kritik*, 17.
Yin, R. (1984): *Case Study Research: Design and Methods*. California: Sage.
Zaner, R. M. (1973): "Solitude and Sociality: The Critical Foundations of the Social Sciences", in *Phenomenological Sociology. Issues and Applications*, G. E. Psathas (ed.). New York: John Wiley, 25-43.

Qualitative methods are increasingly used in market research, evaluation, consultancy, education, and social research. Students in many disciplines use qualitative methods in their reports and dissertations.

However, qualitative research does not always demonstrate a chain of evidence linking conclusions with data. Consultants' reports are often based more on impressions than on presented data. Students spend a long time in preparation of qualitative research, and their analyses are often weak.

This book provides practical advice on how to display qualitative data. It also explains why a display of qualitative data is important in a larger methodological context.

LEONARDO CECCHINI

*Parlare
per le notti*

Il fantastico nell'opera
di Tommaso Landolfi

Etudes Romanes 51